the book of
PROVERBS:
good advice
for
good living

Jealousy is like a
cancer (14:30*b*)

Smart people watch
their step (14:15*b*)

A gentle answer quiets
anger (15:1*a*)

Be careful how you think;
your life is shaped
by your thoughts (4:23)

An arrogant person never
admits he is wrong (13:1*b*)

the book of

PROVERBS:
good advice
for
good living

John H. Scammon

JUDSON PRESS® VALLEY FORGE

To be wise you must first
have reverence for the LORD
(9:10a)

A nagging wife is like
water going drip-drip-drip
(19:13b)

Plan carefully what you do
(4:26a)

The LORD hates people who
use dishonest scales (11:1a)

Anyone who spreads gossip
is a fool (10:18b)

Lazy people should learn a
lesson from the way ants live
(6:6)

These quotations and all other biblical quotations in the book, except where noted, are from the *Good News Bible*—Old Testament: Copyright © American Bible Society 1976; New Testament: Copyright © American Bible Society 1966, 1971, 1976. Used by permission.

Also quoted in this book are:

New American Standard Bible, © The Lockman Foundation 1960, 1962, 1963, 1968, 1971, 1973, 1975, and are used by permission.

The Holy Bible, King James Version.

The New English Bible, copyright © The Delegates of the Oxford University Press and the Syndics of the Cambridge University Press, 1961, 1970.

The Living Bible (Wheaton, Illinois: Tyndale House Publishers, 1971). Used by permission.

From *Proverbs • Ecclesiastes (Anchor Bible),* translated and edited by R. B. Y. Scott: Copyright © 1965 by Doubleday & Company, Inc. Used by permission of the publisher.

The Jerusalem Bible, copyright © 1966 by Darton, Longman & Todd, Ltd., and Doubleday and Company, Inc. Used by permission of the publisher.

The Bible: A New Translation by James Moffatt. Copyright 1954 by James Moffatt. Reprinted by permission of Harper & Row, Publishers, Inc.

Library of Congress Cataloging in Publication Data

Scammon, John H.
  Good advice for good living.

  Includes bibliographical references.
  1. Conduct of life. 2. Bible. O.T. Proverbs —Criticism, interpretation, etc. I. Title.
BJ1581.2.S3   248'.4   78-24505
ISBN 0-8170-0819-5

WHO
  DOES
    NOT
      HEED
        PROVERBS
          WILL
            NOT
              AVOID
                MISTAKES

—Turkish proverb.

Dedication

To my three grandsons, Dave, John, and Andy Sargent, who are my reasons for especially enjoying Proverbs 17:6a; and to the Adult Bible Class of the University Church at Central Philippine University, Iloilo City, Philippines, which met at 7:30 A.M. on Sunday mornings, and whose members aided greatly by discussing many of these topics.

Acknowledgments

I wish to thank the Reverend Edward A. Cline, Associate Secretary of the American Bible Society, for granting most generous permission to quote the *Good News Bible* on so many pages of this book, and the publishers who gave permission to reprint shorter passages. My appreciation also goes to my long-time and valued friend Evan F. Bailey, who read practically all of the manuscript and made helpful suggestions. Three people contributed to the appendix: two former students, Rosalyn Kemp Reiff and Veronica Lanier, who, years ago, prepared extensive term papers on the proverbs of many races and cultures, and Mrs. Marguerite Estaver, who collected pages and pages of English proverbs, mostly contemporary.

I have deeply appreciated the collections and services of the Concord (New Hampshire) Public Library and of the New Hampshire State Library, also the directors of special collections over the country who were of great help in tracking down material.

Finally, to the Reverend Harold L. Twiss, Managing Editor of Judson Press, and to Mrs. Phyllis A. Frantz, Assistant Editor, a very special note of thanks for their help in seeing the manuscript through all the stages until press release—and also for their friendship. And to my wife, who put up with my "idiosnickeries" while I was working on this book, deepest love and thanks.

Contents

Introduction

Recently an amazing thing happened. I picked up the *Living Proverbs* (taken from *The Living Bible*) and opened it at random. My eye fell on the tenth chapter, the nineteenth verse: "Don't talk so much. You keep putting your foot in your mouth. Be sensible and turn off the flow!" Well, this was quite a challenge to one who has earned much of his living by talking!

Billy Graham is reported to read five psalms every day to learn, as he puts it, how to get along with God, and one chapter of the Proverbs to learn how to get along with other people. Certainly there is no other book of the Bible which contains such down-to-earth advice about everyday living as Proverbs. One of my former students in seminary, the Reverend Alan B. Bond, now minister of the Congregational Church (United Church of Christ), Scottsdale, Arizona, wrote in a final examination, "By the way, this is one of my favorite books of the Old Testament. As strange as it may seem, I used this when I was in the service as my moral guide."

Take two or three minutes to make up three proverbs by which a lot of Americans seem to be steering their lives today. What do you think about these as samples:

1. Make a "fast buck" every chance you get; never mind how you do it.

2. Don't work too hard or too fast; prolong coffee breaks and lunch hours, and just do a passably decent job and only where it shows.

3. If *you* don't look out for Number One, nobody else will.

My reasons for writing this little book are five:

1. The book of Proverbs, so jam-packed with advice about the "nitty-gritty" details of life, doesn't get very much attention in Bible study at a time when we need help on these matters more than we have for a long, long time.

2. The book places heavy emphasis on the necessity of a planned, thought-out life, a quality so often lacking today.

3. But Proverbs is not only down-to-earth and practical; it also has a deeply religious slant. The motto of the book is "The fear of the Lord is the beginning of knowledge" (1:7a in both the King James and the Revised Standard Versions).

4. Also, is it possible that a nation and its culture can be sized up by the common, everyday sayings in daily circulation, passed on sometimes from generation to generation?

5. If, as a very famous basketball player (later an equally famous coach) said, "Our American society has become rotten to the core," when are we going to start rebuilding the ideas of truth telling, honesty, morality, decency, and integrity in both high and low places? Might some work on the book of Proverbs help at least some of us?

John H. Scammon
Concord, New Hampshire

Know Some Good Rules
for Living?

Yes, But What
Is a Proverb?

1. "A short, pithy saying in common and recognized use. . . ."—*Oxford English Dictionary*.

2. "Sayings which combine sense, shortness, and salt."—James Howell, *Proverbs,* 1659.

3. "Ginowine proverbs are like good kambrick needles—short, sharp, and shiny."—Josh Billings (pseud. of Henry Wheeler Shaw), 1818–85.

4. "Sense, brevity, and point are the elements of a good proverb."—Tryon Edwards, *Dictionary of Thoughts,* 1891.

5. "Short sayings drawn from long experience."—Cervantes, *Don Quixote,* 1605.

6. "The wisdom of many and the wit of one." (Also quoted as "A proverb is one man's wit and all men's wisdom.")—Lord John Russell, *Apothegm, ca.* 1850.

7. "A short, pithy saying, presenting in striking form a well-known truth."—*Encyclopedia Americana*.

8. "It is anonymous, traditional, and epigrammatic."—Archer Taylor, *The Proverb,* 1931.

9. "Strictly speaking, an epigram, an aphorism, or a maxim does not qualify as proverbial unless it has passed into common use."—*The Anchor Bible*.

1
Lying: Should One EVER Lie?

Jim Brown, an engineer who has been out of work for months and who has a family dependent on him, is being interviewed for a good opening.

"How old?" asks the personnel man.

"Forty-six," replies Jim,

"Sorry. You'd be OK for the job, but my orders are to get a man forty-five or under. Sorry."

Jim leaves the office grumbling to himself, "I should have lied. Should have said forty-four. I'd have had the job, and I surely need it!"

• • •

Dr. Smith is making his rounds in the hospital. Mrs. Brown, a young patient, has been operated on for possible cancer the day before, and the surgeon has discovered that her body is full of the disease. She is an extremely high-strung, nervous woman, and now waits for Dr. Smith's report. Her body is weak from yesterday's ordeal. Her eyes anxiously search the surgeon's face. "Tell me, doctor, am I going to get well?" He thinks fast. Worried for fear that she will go to pieces if he tells the whole truth, he replies, "You are going to come along. We will do everything we can, and you must be optimistic."

Exactly What Is a Lie?

We had better find out, before going further, what a lie really is. The dictionaries agree that it is an untrue statement which is made with a deliberate intent to deceive someone. But they also suggest that a person may *act* a lie without saying anything. What's more, some dictionaries have a definition of a "white" lie; this is a false or untrue statement which is made to be polite or kind, that is, to shield someone from unpleasant truth. (You may ask at once, "Is this just as bad as a 'regular' lie?")

Let's go further and ask,

✓ Are half-truths lies?

✓ Is it possible that there are *many* shades of lies, some of which are minor? Or are they all equally bad?

Are There Some Proverbs About This?

Let's emphasize that one problem about reading the book of Proverbs is that usually *many* different subjects are brought up in the course of one chapter. (Try counting all the topics mentioned in a typical section.)

Take six minutes to read and think about the following passages in Proverbs:

a. "There are seven things that the LORD hates and cannot tolerate:

A proud look,

a lying tongue,

hands that kill innocent people,

a mind that thinks up wicked plans,

feet that hurry off to do evil,

a witness who tells one lie after another,

and a man who stirs up trouble among friends" (6:16, 19). [Italics mine.]

b. "A man who hides his hatred is a liar" (10:18*a*).

c. "When you tell the truth, justice is done, but lies lead to injustice" (12:17).

d. "A lie has a short life, but truth lives on forever" (12:19). (Raise questions whenever you see fit.)

e. "The LORD hates liars, but is pleased with those who keep their word" (12:22).

f. "Honest people hate lies, but the words of wicked people are shameful and disgraceful" (13:5).

g. "A reliable witness always tells the truth, but an unreliable one tells nothing but lies" (14:5).

h. "A witness saves lives when he tells the truth; when he tells lies, he betrays people" (14:25).

i. "Respected people do not tell lies, and fools have nothing worthwhile to say" (17:7).

j. "If you tell lies in court, you will be punished—there will be no escape" (19:5).

k. "No one who tells lies in court can escape punishment; he is doomed" (19:9).

l. "You have to hate someone to want to hurt him with lies. Insincere talk brings nothing but ruin" (26:28).

m. "I ask you, God, to let me have two things before I die; keep me from lying, and let me be neither rich nor poor" (30:7, 8*a*).

PUT A CHECK MARK BEFORE THE ONES YOU APPROVE OF MOST STRONGLY. Do you wish to qualify any? For example, did this thought come into your mind when you read some of them: "Is this *always* the way things work out in my experience and in the world in which I live?"

We Need to Go Deeper Now

Put into your own words what the passages in the previous section say. It might be something like this:

(a) and *(e)* tell us that God hates lying.

(d) claims that truth outlasts lies.

(f) says that honesty and lying have nothing to do with each other.

(g), *(j)*, and *(k)* condemn those who lie when they are called in as court witnesses.

(m) is an earnest prayer that one may not give in to the temptation to lie.

YOU MAY NOTICE THAT ALL OF THESE PASSAGES SO FAR PUT A BLACK MARK AGAINST LYING—BUT THEY DO NOT GIVE REASONS. However, *(b)*, *(c)*, *(h)*, *(i)*, and *(l)* may help here.

(b) and *(l)* (which, incidentally, are both difficult to translate) each connect lying with hatred. (How often is this true as you observe life?)

(c) says that lies are one cause of injustice in our world.

(h) emphasizes that lying in court may cause the ruin of another person.

(i) says that a liar cannot be respected.

So, HERE ARE AT LEAST FOUR STRIKES (three are usually enough) against lies and lying:

1. Lies sometimes originate in human hatred.

2. Lying often causes rank injustice to someone else.
3. Lies in court have often ruined others.
4. Lies hurt people!

Keep on with Some More Questions

✓ Why do children lie to their parents?
✓ Why do parents lie to their children?
✓ Do politicians in high places sometimes lie? Why?
✓ Is cheating on one's income tax return a case of lying? What if you shade the figures only a little bit?
✓ What do you observe to be the commonest forms of lying?
✓ Is failing to tell the whole truth the same as lying?

Try an Imaginary Experiment

In order to find all available answers to our many questions, try to imagine that in your own home, beginning the next hour on the hour, every single member of your family, for twenty-four hours, will tell nothing but lies to one another. Imagine conversations between the various members, raise questions that different family members might ask, and go on with answers which, in each case, are deliberate untruths. TAKE SOME MINUTES ON THIS and get at important, crucial family matters. Then suppose that at the end of the twenty-four hours there is a family council, and that now all are sworn to tell the truth. How do you think everything would come out? What effect would be produced?

Can We Get Help from Books on Ethics?

Books on the subject of ethics call attention to two groups of people: those who say, "You must tell the absolute truth, cost what it may," and those who maintain that we owe the truth only to those who are entitled to it (i.e., not to gossips, international spies, etc.) and to those who are able to bear it (not the dangerously ill person). One book which I consulted goes on to caution that most of us err on the side of those who, for various reasons, find excuses for veering from the truth. Take time to get a good book on ethics from your public library and read the pages on truth telling and lying.

At Last, Some Answers?

Let's go back to Proverbs 6:16: "There are seven things that the LORD hates and cannot tolerate . . . a lying tongue." Put in your own words several possible answers to the question, "Exactly what do you mean when you say that God hates lying?" Here are some possibilities:

✓ God has put us into a world where the kind of living which is based on deceit and lies is INTOLERABLE.

✓ Any satisfactory life with others (family, friends, business associates) is based on mutual trust.

✓ Lies, either told or acted, are invariably followed by a breakdown in confidence and understanding—the things which help so much to make living happy.

✓ Some lies are caused by unsocial personality characteristics (such as desire to evade someone or something), by dislike, even by hatred (look back now to 10:18a and 26:28a).

✓ In other words, a world, or a community, or a family of liars represents the height of unhappiness.

And if there are a very few exceptions when not telling the truth may be the lesser of two evils, even that does not make it right; a lie is still a lie and therefore a very serious matter in the eyes of God. And our discussion must surely end with our Lord's words, "Do not swear at all, either by *heaven* . . . or by *the earth* . . . or . . . by your own head either. . . . All you need say is 'Yes' if you mean yes, 'No' if you mean no" (Matthew 5:34-37, *Jerusalem Bible*). In other words, the Christian is one whose word can be trusted, completely and invariably. That is a large order!

And if telling the strict truth is to become a mark of normal life again, both individually and nationally, it has to begin somewhere— why not with you and me?

How Do You React to This?

Trade Mark Registered
A McNaught Syndicate Feature

What Some Others Have Said

"Little children do not lie till they are taught to do so."—Saadia ben Joseph, *Letter,* A.D. 928.

"One of the most startling differences between a cat and a lie is that a cat has only nine lives."—Mark Twain, *Pudd'nhead Wilson's Calendar,* 1893.

"He who permits himself to tell a lie once, finds it much easier to do it a second and third time, till at length it becomes habitual."—Thomas Jefferson, *Letter to Peter Carr,* 1785.

"He who tells a lie, is not sensible of how great a task he undertakes; for he must be forced to invent twenty more to maintain that one."—Alexander Pope, *Thoughts on Various Subjects,* 1727.

"This is the punishment of a liar: he is not believed, even when he speaks the truth."—Babylonian Talmud: *Sanhedrin,* 89*b.*

"The cruelest lies are often told in silence."—Robert Louis Stevenson, *Virginibus Puerisque: Truth of Intercourse,* 1874.

"It is better to be lied about than to lie."—Elbert Hubbard, *The Philistine,* July, 1900.

"Half the truth is often a great lie."—Benjamin Franklin, *Poor Richard's Almanack,* July, 1758.

"Nothing can need a lie."—George Herbert (1593-1633), *The Church-Porch.*

2

Why Does Gossiping Seem So Much Fun?

"Gossip is so tasty—how we love to swallow it!" (Proverbs 18:8).

> *"More people are run down by gossip than by automobiles."* [1]

A friend once told me of an influential layman who didn't like his minister. In fact, he wanted to force him to leave that church. What technique do you think he followed to get the minister out? Whenever he met other church members, he made one short comment. He never went further in the discussion if he could avoid it. This is what he said: "Things aren't right in our church, are they?" He said it over and over again. It was enough. Finally the minister had to resign.

• • •

A high school student needs a summer job very badly. During spring vacation he locates one in the local drugstore where business always picks up during the summer months. He feels greatly relieved to have the job situation settled.

But there is another high school youngster who has had his eye on that job. When he hears that the other boy has been hired, he starts a campaign. It doesn't take too many conversations. In fact, he never goes directly to the drugstore owner. He just lets brief rumors of little dishonesties at school, which he manufactures out of whole cloth, slip

[1] Salada Tea tag line used with permission of the Kellogg Company.

through to the owner second or thirdhand. He makes sure that the rumors are the "hush-hush" variety which won't get back to the original applicant for the job. The result: the boy who has been hired is called in and the contract broken, but only for concocted reasons which hide the real one.

Exactly What Is Gossip?

Here are a couple of dictionary definitions: "Idle talk; groundless rumor"; "familiar or idle talk; groundless rumor; mischievous tattle." And one who gossips is one who "runs from house to house or goes about tattling and telling news." Let's add a definition of gossip which was quoted in a friend's church calendar: "Gossip is giving information of a personal nature to those who are neither a part of the problem nor a part of the solution."

In a summer conference we did some role playing to illustrate how a story can grow through gossipy retelling. Act 1 shows the close of the devotional period at the Women's Union meeting; the pastor is leading it. (This might take place equally well in the Men's Club.) The minister announces that he is on his way to the hospital to see Mr. Brown (a prominent parishioner); he tells the group he does not know why Mr. Brown is in the hospital, only that he is there. As he leaves, the women break up into four activity groups (knitting, White Cross, needlework, and pottery). Each group begins to raise possibilities about Mr. Brown, and choice gossip about his business and family problems follow. How the juicy tidbits come in!

In act 2 we follow the pastor to the hospital; he discovers that Mr. Brown is to have a run-of-the-mill appendicitis operation. After a pleasant chat and a prayer, the pastor leaves.

Act 3 is located in Mr. Brown's home the next morning. Mail begins to pour in. Activity group number 1 sends a letter hoping that Mr. Brown's tests will prove negative and not show any trace of leukemia! Mrs. Brown is horrified! Where did the idea of leukemia ever originate?

The second activity group sends a generous offer to help. If there is a family problem, the note states gently, the local Family Service Bureau is excellent; another couple in the church received no end of help there last year when the husband and wife went through a time of strained relationship. Mrs. Brown was horrified at the first note, but thoroughly angered at this one!

The third group's letter suggests in a friendly way that if Mr. Brown is worried about business difficulties, there is the possibility of a small loan from the Church Contingency Fund to tide him over; or, doesn't the government have loans for small businesses? (You can imagine the look on Mrs. Brown's face now.)

And the fourth group, having turned on the radio as the two-hour activity program ends, catches the last bit of an announcement of the death of a prominent citizen, doesn't get the name, jumps to the conclusion that it is Mr. Brown, and sends Mrs. Brown flowers; they express hope that the entire Women's Union can attend the funeral service in a body!

The impromptu skit ends with a scene at noon. Mrs. Brown's phone is ringing; it is Mr. Brown! He is out of anesthesia, feels good, and wants to notify his wife himself that everything is fine.

Are There Some Helpful Proverbs About Gossip?

Well, I guess there are! Right off we find two identical verses in the book (18:8 and 26:22). In *The Living Bible* they are slightly different from each other but are very forcefully stated as follows: "What dainty morsels rumors are. They are eaten with great relish!" and "Gossip is a dainty morsel eaten with great relish." Let's look at this verse more closely.

The Hebrew original of the two verses is identical; word by word, it can be translated, "Words of a slanderer (or whisperer), what is eaten greedily (some take what has been said so far as meaning that what is said is mysterious, or that it is wounding); and they go down chambers (or recesses) of the belly (or womb, or innermost part)." You can see that the text is difficult. The King James Version has, "The words of a talebearer are as wounds, and they go down into the innermost parts of the belly." But the *New American Standard Bible* reads, "The words of a whisperer are like dainty morsels, and they go down into the innermost parts of the body." Compare this with what was quoted above from *The Living Bible*. So, although the verse is not easy to translate, nevertheless the gist is clear: gossip is something of a tempting, juicy morsel.

One problem that we face in dealing with gossip in the book of Proverbs is that different translations use different words while referring to the same thing. Study this chart for five minutes:

	King James	New American Standard	New English Bible
10:18b	slander	slander	calumny
16:28	whisperer	slanderer	tale-bearing
18:8+26:22	talebearer	whisperer	gossip's whispers
20:19	talebearer	slanderer gossip in 19b	gossip tattler in 19b
25:23	backbiting tongue	backbiting tongue	slander
26:20	talebearer	whisperer	tale-bearer

	Jerusalem Bible	Living Bible	Good News Bible
10:18b	slander	slander	spreads gossip
16:28	talebearer	gossip	gossip is spread
18:8+26:22	talebearer	rumors	gossip
20:19	bearer of gossip chatterers in 19b	gossip in 26:22 gossip	gossip
25:23	backbiting tongue	retort	gossip
26:20	talebearer	gossip	gossip

(Notice how the Elizabethan term "backbite" has practically dropped out of use now.)

Let's get down to "pay dirt." Try putting the above verses into your own words. Here are possibilities:

10:18—simply characterizes the gossiper.

16:28—gossip hurts relationships.

18:8 and 26:22—the attraction of gossiping for some folks is stated.

20:19—gossip undermines reliability.

25:23—gossiping about people can make them very angry.

26:20—gossip also causes arguments.

Let's put it this way for a trial rule for living: Whatever strengthens human relationships may be told, if you sincerely believe it is true. Whatever hurts relationships must NOT be passed on. As Blaise Pascal put it, ". . . if all men knew what each said of the other, there would not be four friends in the world."[2]

And

"If we only said of others
    What we'd say face to face,
A lot of conversation
    Would never take place."[3]

[2] *Pensées*, sec. 2, no. 101 (*ca.* 1660).
[3] Author unknown. Found in the *Sarum Primer*, 1558.

The New Testament says, ". . . speaking the truth in love, we are to grow up in every way into him who is the head, into Christ . . ." (Ephesians 4:15, RSV).

Further Questions for Discussion

1. Does this mean that we must always say complimentary things about other people?
2. Does it mean we must never say anything disparaging?
3. How much news should we spread?
4. What do you think of the Salada Tea tag line, "Learn from the parrot—repeat only what you hear; don't make a story out of it"?[4] How safe is this is rule?
5. Or this anonymous saying, "Gossips try to find out what neighbors do—friends try to understand why"?

We might well close with those famous words,

> "God be in my head,
> And in my understanding;
>
> .   .   .
>
> God be in my mouth,
> And in my speaking."[5]

What Some Others Have Said

"Gossip is vice enjoyed vicariously."—Elbert Hubbard, *The Philistine,* vol. 19, August, 1904.

"Scandalmonger: one who puts who and who together and gets whew!"—Source unknown.

"*They say so,* is half a lie."—Thomas Fuller, *Gnomologia,* 1732.

"That which passes out of one mouth passes into a hundred ears."— Ernest Bramah, *Kai Lung's Golden Hours,* 1923.

"A cruel story runs on wheels, and every hand oils the wheels as they run."—Ouida (pseud. of Louise Ramée, later de la Ramé), *Wisdom, Wit and Pathos, ca.* 1880.

"No mud can soil us but the mud we throw."—James Russell Lowell, (1819–1891), letter to George William Curtis.

"With two eyes and one tongue you should see twice as much as you

[4]Salada Tea tag line used with permission of the Kellogg Company.
[5]Author unknown.

say."—Salada Tea tag line. Used with permission of the Kellogg Company.

"There are two good rules which ought to be written on every heart—never to believe anything bad about anybody unless you positively know it to be true; never to tell even that unless you feel that it is absolutely necessary and that God is listening while you tell it."—Source unknown.

3

The Nagging Wife—
But What About
the Nagging Husband?

A middle-aged salesman, looking very harried, said to the counselor in family relations: "My wife gives me no peace. No matter what I do for her, no matter how much I try to please her, she keeps nagging and hassling me."

● ● ●

Again, Jim B. has three "pet peeves," and he reminds his wife on every possible occasion that she is doing at least one of them: (1) she is spending too much money on her clothes; (2) she is always late in getting the meals on the table (unlike his mother); and (3) she always keeps him waiting when they go out together.

But before we go further we had better ask, *"Exactly what* is nagging?" Dictionaries claim that the word is related to both Old Norse and Old English words meaning, "to gnaw." Does that help? Check the words below which come closest to what the word means to you:

To irritate by constant mentioning.
To annoy by bringing up the same subject over and over again.
"Harping on the same old string."
Hounding or badgering.

WARNING

Be careful about reading this chapter, especially the verses in the book of Proverbs dealing with nagging. The reason: This is the easiest book in the Bible to read and then say, "I just wish So-and-so could read that!" Don't do it!

Here are four vivid references to start us off; we are going to take a hard look at each one:

"A nagging wife is like water going drip-drip-drip" (19:13*b*).

"It is better to live in the corner of an attic than with a crabby woman in a lovely home" (21:9, *The Living Bible*).

"Better to live out in the desert than with a nagging, complaining wife" (21:19).

"A nagging wife is like water going drip-drip-drip on a rainy day. How can you keep her quiet? Have you ever tried to stop the wind or ever tried to hold a handful of oil?" (27:15, 16).

WELL !!

Take a moment and ask yourself:

1. Does reading these verses make me angry?

2. For women—Is my immediate reaction, "Why doesn't the author mention nagging husbands?"

3. For men—Do I *(a)* agree completely with the statements, or *(b)* agree that SOME women nag, or *(c)* want to defend wives?

Try an Experiment

Would it be thought-provoking to change one word in each of the four statements? Since the original author lived many centuries ago (when it was a man's world), try reading aloud the four passages in Proverbs but *put in* "husband" each time the text reads "wife."

Add a fifth statement that does not lay the blame on either party: "A dry crust eaten in peace is better than steak every day along with argument and strife" (17:1, *The Living Bible*).

Now ask yourself two questions and add to the answers that are suggested for each:

1. What things is a husband most likely to nag his wife about?

✓ What she spends on clothes.

✓ Time spent away from home (clubs, circles, teas, political discussion groups, etc.).

✓ Running up the charge accounts.

✓ Wasting time gossiping on the phone.

✓ _____

✓ _____

✓ _____

2. What things is a wife most likely to nag her husband about?

✓ Being out too many evenings without her.

✓ Paying too much attention to the opposite sex.

✓ Unwillingness to take more responsibility in bringing up the children.

✓ Leaving his stuff around the house in a messy way.

✓ Stinking up the house with cigar smoke.

✓ _____

✓ _____

✓ _____

✓ _____

A Skit?

Are you in a position where you and a friend of the opposite sex (preferably your spouse) can work up a 10-minute skit involving nagging? If so, it may give you a long, hard look at the real "anatomy" of this matter. Present it at some appropriate function to open a discussion of the subject.

Test Yourself

Now suppose you'd like to test yourself: "How to Tell Whether or Not I Qualify as a Nagger." Here are eight questions; mark each one conscientiously before moving to the next one. Give each a number, from 1 to 4, meaning

                1. Very often

                2. Now and then

                3. Rarely

                4. Never

✓ How many times in the past week have I "casually" mentioned AGAIN something I wish he/she would get around to doing one of these days?	Mark 1, 2, 3, or 4
✓ Has anyone ever told you that you "pick" at your spouse?	
✓ How often have I asked my spouse for something which he/she thinks I don't need, but *I* feel I do?	

✓ When I see something I don't like in my partner, but which isn't really important, how often do I just dismiss it without a mention?	
✓ Can I think of some person whom I regard as a first-class nagger? Now have I, in the last month, done any of the things which I note in the other person?	
✓ How often do I say to my husband/wife, "Now BE SURE . . ."?	
✓ What is my PET peeve in regard to my partner? How many times have I mentioned it to him/her this past week?	
✓ How often do I refer to something my spouse did in the past which both of us agree was a mistake?	

Let's Admit

If we are going to be fair, we must admit that nagging can sometimes be explained by circumstances, such as ill health, an unhappy childhood, or ill treatment. But we are not so much concerned with explaining it as expunging it!

Let's also admit that honest, friendly criticism is NOT what we are talking about ("It is a badge of honor to accept valid criticism"— Proverbs 25:12, *The Living Bible*); we ARE concerned with *repeated, annoying* criticism.

Now we are ready for some constructive "ways out." Does the book of Proverbs help on this? Reread the four proverbs quoted at the beginning of this chapter. The first thing we notice is that these verses LAY DOWN STATEMENTS; they do not provide solutions. Doesn't the book, then, help at all? Yes. In all fairness to wives, we should say, loudly and clearly, that the NAGGING wife isn't the only kind of wife described in the book. Chapter 31:10-31 gives the author's clear picture of the IDEAL wife. Take time to read the passage. What are your impressions?

1. _____

2. _____

3. _____

4. _____

But notice that the verses describe what she *does* more than what she *is;* only one verse, 25, may help on this. "She is strong and respected and not afraid of the future." And see what her husband says about her in verse 29. And, husbands, look up 18:22; how long has it been since you said a few words of real appreciation to your helpmeet?

But we still need *down-to-earth, practical* suggestions as to how a nagger can "cut it out."

At the beginning of this chapter we quoted four *statements;* here are four other passages to place on a side of the sheet which we might call HELPS TOWARD A SOLUTION:

STATEMENT	SOLUTION
1. 19:13*b*	1. 12:18
2. 21:9	2. 15:1*a*
3. 21.19	3. 15:23
4. 27:15, 16	4. 17:9*a*

BE SURE TO READ THESE, preferably aloud, and in a modern translation. And put down below three or four ways in which they suggest very specific ways to stop nagging:

_____

_____

_____

Let's end with the kind of recommendations which marriage counselors suggest in our popular magazines and in "Dear Abby" columns in the newspaper. Also there are some helpful books now which advise on ways to ensure a more permanent marriage.

Recommendation 1. Learn to recognize nagging when you are doing it. And, if your partner accuses you, rather than "flying off the handle" and serving up a tart reply, check to see if it is true.

Recommendation 2. If *you* are the nagger (or one of them), ask yourself if there is a more effective way to accomplish what you have in mind. Just possibly, nagging will result in making your partner more determined than ever to do just the opposite of what you wish.

Recommendation 3. Try to list in your own mind (or in a heatless discussion) what the chief topics are about which BOTH of you nag. And from there go on to ask if you both may not be "blowing off steam" more than really trying to accomplish worthwhile objectives.

Recommendation 4. How long since you have given a few words of generous praise to your partner for something which you really do appreciate? As one writer puts it, "One cannot change the 'inside' of a person by continual hammering upon the 'outside.'"[1]

Recommendation 5. This recommendation is as important as several of the others put together. When nagging occurs, try to give it a humorous turn. Dr. A. J. Cronin tells in his autobiography of spending a dismal day in the rain as a young doctor in Wales. When he came home, famished, to his young bride in the evening, she cooked him *one egg* which proved to be spoiled! Then he let loose with all appropriate (and inappropriate) words and phrases, and she matched them until, suddenly, they looked into each other's angry eyes, broke out into wild laughter, and embraced![2]

Does all or even some of this help? For us Christians, if Christ is in the home, there are some things that get crowded out. Nagging is one of them.

"How Wonderful It Is to Be Able to Say the Right Thing at the Right Time!"

PROVERBS 15:23b (The Living Bible)

---

[1] H. A. Bowman, *Marriage for Moderns* (New York: McGraw-Hill, 1965), p. 410.
[2] A. J. Cronin, *Adventures in Two Worlds* (Boston: Little, Brown and Company, 1956), p. 242.

4
How to
Bring Up Boys

> *"Isn't it strange that people without children bring them up so well?"*[1]

Never before have we had so many books on raising children! Here are a few titles:

How to Bring up a Child Without Spending a Fortune

How to Get a Teen-Age Boy & What to Do with Him When You Get Him

Today's Teen

The Feeling Child

Parents & Children, Love & Discipline

Let's Plunge Right In

Does the book of Proverbs help on this problem? It certainly has a lot to say! We have been working all along on the theory that no other book of the Bible contains so much down-to-earth, practical advice on the "nitty-gritty" problems of everyday living as this one. Is this true?

There are at least forty-eight passages on the subject of raising boys! Please take time to read them; each one has a different slant:

1:8—Listening to Father and Mother

1:10-19—What vicious company can do

2:20—On having heroes

3:11—Figuring what God is doing with you

4:5, 10, 11—Remembering what your father tells you about how to live

[1] Salada Tea tag line used with permission of the Kellogg Company.

4:13—The danger of forgetting what you've learned
4:14-17—The effect of bum friends
4:20, 21—Father knows best
6:20—Same thought as 1:8
7:2, 3—Same as 4:5
10:1—Parents do have feelings
11:29—The result of making trouble for your family
13:1—Do you believe in discipline? How much?
13:22—Money for grandchildren?
13:24—More on discipline
14:26—Religion and family life
15:5—Not ignoring what Father said and did
15:20—Again, parents have feelings, don't they?
17:6—When each member of the family is proud of the others
17:16—Worth spending on their education?
17:21—When Dad feels badly
17:25—The pains of parenthood
19:13—How to ruin Father
19:18—How permissive shall we be?
19:26—What are children doing to parents?
19:27—Is misused instruction worse than none?
20:7—When kids are lucky
20:20—Is this really done?
20:29—When hair gets gray
22:6—Starting early
22:15—On spanking
23:13, 14—More of the same
23:15, 16—What makes parents proud?
23:19—Serious thoughts about life?
23:20—On associating with heavy eaters and heavy drinkers
23:22—Listening and appreciating
23:24—When Dad feels good
23:25—Let Dad and Mother both feel good
24:3—What are homes built on?
27:11—Same idea as in 23:24
28:7—Law-abiding sons?
28:24—Who'd do this?
29:3—Same idea as 23:24
29:15—When a youngster always has his/her own way
29:17—More on discipline

30:17—Making fun of your father and despising your old mother
31:27—What good mothers do
31:28, 29—Appreciating Mother

A Carload of Questions

Immediately stacks and stacks of questions pop into our minds, such as:

✓ Why doesn't the book of Proverbs ever mention bringing up daughters (unless there is a hint in chapter 31)?

✓ Does advice given well over two thousand years ago on this subject have much relevance in the 1970s?

✓ Isn't it harder to raise youngsters today than ever before?

✓ What about broken homes in which one parent has the sole responsibility?

✓ Are parents much too permissive today?

✓ Does the Bible really give us specific answers to most of the daily problems we face today? If not, why not?

✓ Have *you* brought up *your* children differently from the way *your* parents brought *you* up?

And you can probably add two or three more; please write them down:

1. _____

_____

2. _____

_____

Misconception Number One

Right off we see that there is really *nothing fundamentally new in the problems surrounding the raising of youngsters to be responsible adults.* In fact, about four thousand years ago in Egypt, Ptah-hotep, a leading official of the king, left some writings in which he instructed his son in the way to grow up in order to prepare for a responsible position. His advice may be summed up as follows: The son must be "teachable, modest, self-controlled, reliable, honest, respectful to superiors, and of good moral behavior. Above all, he must order his life according to justice and truth . . ." *(Anchor Bible).*

To be sure, *gadgets* change generation after generation but not youngsters. It is perfectly possible to make a strong case that high-speed cars, available drugs, a lowered legal drinking age, and increasing sexual freedom *complicate* the situation. But fundamental drives and ambitions don't change over the generations. Do you agree?

Indeed, in an even more famous writing, another Egyptian official, Amen-em-ope, addressed (probably before 1000 B.C.) thirty sections of advice which are remarkably similar to Proverbs 22:17–23:11 to his youngest son. Was Amen-em-ope influenced by a well-known piece of literature?

Perhaps it would be worth three minutes of recollection of some of the things OUR parents faced when they were bringing US up.

Now, can the forty-eight quotations we found be hung on pegs in some sort of order? Let's divide them as follows:

1. What the book says about fathers, and
2. What it says about sons.

PARENTHETICALLY,

daughters are not mentioned because it was a man's world, and girls were brought up to be wives and to bear children. Sons were regarded as special objects of training because they would carry the burden of work out in the world, and they would also carry on the family name. (Some scholars have doubted that public instruction was ever afforded to daughters.)

What the Book Says About Fathers

The first impression that one gets from the passages as a unit is that fathers *have a job to do with their boys which nobody else can ever quite carry out.*

The *Good News Bible* translates 6:20, "Son, do what your father tells you and never forget what your mother taught you." But *exactly what* is the division of labor here? Plaut, a very helpful Jewish commentator, says that the father handles the rules of practical, everyday life *(mitsvot)* while the mother imparts the general principles which underlie one's existence.[2] Try several translations here.

Certainly all through the book of Proverbs the idea that the father is a powerful example in the life of a boy is expressed. ". . . Boys are proud of their fathers" (17:6b).

[2] W. G. Plaut, *Book of Proverbs, A Commentary* (New York: Union of American Hebrew Congregations, 1961), p. 91. Reprinted by permission of the publisher, the Union of American Hebrew Congregations.

A recent survey conducted by the University of Southern California finds that in the majority of the two thousand families studied, fathers determined the religious behavior of their children more than mothers did. If a father goes to church regularly, for example, *no matter whether the mother does or not,* the youngsters are also likely to attend regularly.

A second word which comes through about fathers over and over again is that *the disciplining of sons is not an option;* IT IS A MUST. Read the following passages, preferably aloud: 13:24; 15:5; 19:18; 22:15; 23:13, 14; 29:15; and 29:17. As Plaut puts it in his commentary, "The strict parent is the traditional image of the good parent. Extended permissiveness, found in so-called 'modern' homes, would have been viewed with amazement and disapproval by the teacher of Proverbs."[3]

QUESTIONS

When should we use physical punishment?

Are there cases where it should never be used?

If you are a parent struggling with the question of punishment, have you (1) talked with other parents, and (2) consulted some of the excellent books in public libraries on the subject? The book of Proverbs does not go into details.

A third observation: *some fathers tried hard but failed in those days just as they do today.* See 17:21; 17:25; 19:13a. What father does not wish he had done a better job? We all have some regrets and some joys, too. But how our hearts go out to one whose seventeen-year-old boy, who had been in and out of jail, in his last imprisonment wrote farewells in his cell and then hanged himself. This was his note to his father.

"Dad, I sure wish me and you could have understood each other better. But don't feel bad, I still wouldn't trade you for any other. I love you."[4]

So, every day is Father's Day!

How About Sons?

First, *the boy's friends can make him or break him.* So a young man is warned to keep out of the company of racketeers. See the vivid

[3] *Ibid.,* p. 92.
[4] *Mentor,* February, 1962. Published by the inmates, Massachusetts Correctional Institution, Walpole.

description of life among the hoodlums which still attracts capable young men (1:10-19). Then the youth had better keep out of the red light district. What a description of a seductress and her inexperienced victim is in 7:6-27!

And what about the young man who is already married (Jewish youth often married at 17)? He must watch out for the fast-living, sex-obsessed wife who has no regard for her marriage vows. See 2:16-19; all of chapter 5 (and is it vivid!); and 6:24-35; 7:5.

Again, *don't associate with heavy eaters* (gluttons) *and heavy drinkers* (23:20, 21). Note the extremely accurate description of what some of this does to a man in 23:29-35.

Also, *remember that parents have feelings* (over and over again; see, e.g., 17:21, 25). Don't ruin your parents' happiness in their later years!

Who could steal from his parents (28:24) or ridicule them in their old age (30:17)? (There are many ways of doing both of these.)

"A young man who obeys the law is intelligent" (28:7*a*).

And finally, the son is encouraged to continue to learn (19:27).

For both fathers and sons, the words are appropriate which are carved on the outside wall of a certain junior high school: "There never is a day when it is not worth your while to be at your best."

What Some Others Have Said

"A boy has two jobs. One is just being a boy. The other is growing up to be a man."—Herbert Hoover, address on the 50th anniversary celebration of the Boys' Clubs of America, May 21, 1956.

"There must always be a struggle between a father and son, while one aims at power and the other at independence."—Samuel Johnson, in Boswell's *Life of Johnson,* July 14, 1763.

"There are no living experts on the subject of raising boys. There are a lot of students of the subject, but no experts."—W. C. Skousen, *So You Want to Raise a Boy?* 1962.

"I tell you there's a wall ten feet thick and ten miles high between parent and child."—George Bernard Shaw, *Misalliance,* 1914. Used by permission of the Society of Authors, London, on behalf of the Bernard Shaw estate.

"Children need models rather than critics."—Joseph Joubert, *Pensées,* 1842.

"A father is a banker provided by nature."—French proverb.

"It is a wise father that knows his own child."—William Shakespeare, *The Merchant of Venice.*

"A ragged colt may prove a good horse."—Scottish proverb.

"What the world wants iz good examples, not so mutch advice."—Josh Billings (pseud. of Henry Wheeler Shaw), *Complete Works,* 1876.

5

Who Are
the Smart People
and Who Are
the Stupid?

How would you answer the question in the title of this chapter right off the cuff? Are the answers below (1) always right; (2) often right, (3) good as far as they go but inadequate for a universal definition; or (4) what?

"Stupid people are careless and act too quickly" (Proverbs 14:16b).
"Intelligent people are always eager and ready to learn" (18:15).
"Sensible people will see trouble coming and avoid it" (22:3a).
"Stupid people always think they are right" (12:15a).
"Sensible people always think before they act" (13:16a).
"A fool does not care whether he understands a thing or not" (18:2a).
"Smart people watch their step" (14:15b).
"Any fool can start arguments" (20:3a).
"Smart people will ignore an insult" (12:16b).

What Do You Think of the Following?

After years of painstaking research, a scientific investigator discovered a medical formula which was certain to be very valuable in treating disease. An offer of $3,000,000 for the exclusive use of the formula was not long in coming. What did he do? He refused the offer and turned the discovery over, free, to the medical profession in order to hasten wide distribution of the new knowledge. Then he went on

45

with his researches, living, as before, in what we would call anything but luxury.[1]

Now ask again, "Who are the smart people and who are the stupid?" The above story was told in a suburban church to a high school group. One young person had just one word for it, spoken under his breath: "Stupid!"

Raise some questions about the researcher:

✓ Why did he react as he did to the offer?

✓ Could he not have advanced his work further and faster if he had accepted the money and used it for equipment and a large staff?

✓ Did he really succeed in helping more people by turning down the money?

What would a top Madison Avenue advertising man say? A college senior? A local politician? A newspaper reporter? Your doctor? A housewife? Your minister? WHAT DO YOU SAY?

Who is the smartest (in the best sense) person you have ever known?

Help in the Book of Proverbs?

How many times do you suppose the word "wise" occurs in Proverbs? Fifty-nine, in the RSV. How many times does the word "fool" appear? Forty. In addition, other related words like "wisdom," and "foolishness" are found in Proverbs.

First, the Portrait of a Fool

Five different Hebrew words are used in Proverbs, all with the general meaning of "fool," "foolish," "folly," "foolishly," and "foolishness." We must study all five.

The first word is 'ᵉvil (no relation to the English). To pronounce the Hebrew, hurry over the first syllable and put the accent on the last, with the "i" as in "machine." This word is used to describe an unenlightened person, a simpleton who can't be taught and usually one who doesn't have too many moral compunctions. Such a person—

1. "looks down the nose" at wisdom and has no use for advice or instruction (1:7b);

2. sneers at the idea of sin (14:9 in the King James Version; the *New American Standard* has "fools mock at sin");

[1] Benjamin Rush, *Road to Fulfillment* (New York: Harper & Row, Publishers, 1942), p. 170. Rush knew the man.

3. is at the point where trying to teach him is a sheer waste of time (27:22);

4. quarrels a lot (20:3).

Even more often is the second word used. It is *kᵉsil,* again with the accent on the second syllable and the "i" as in "machine." The fool here is *the stupid one,* who—

1. has no use for knowledge (1:22b);

2. thinks wrongdoing is a kind of sport (10:23);

3. "shoots off his mouth" with nonsense (12:23b);

4. throws off restraint and is careless (14:16b, RSV).

Ever know anyone with some of these characteristics?

The third word is *peti* (pronounced "pet-tee," accent on the first syllable). This describes a gullible simpleton; usually there is something of a bad connotation. These people are—

1. very happy to remain just as they are (1:22a);

2. absolutely opposed to learning anything (1:22c);

3. rather inexperienced and easily enticed (1:32a);

4. very complacent (1:24-25).

The fourth word is *hᵃsar lebh* (pronounced with a guttural "h" and a hurried "a" sound after it; accent is on the "sar." The second word: like "lave"). Literally, it means "lacking in heart," but since the Hebrew often thought of his heart as we think of the mind, the phrase really means "lacking in understanding." The vivid description of the way a prostitute seduces a young man (7:6-27) has this word in 7:7b; a good translation would be "senseless."

The fifth word is *nabhal* (pronounced "nahvall" with the accent on the second syllable); it describes one who is mentally dull and also lacking in moral sensitivity, the dull one, who lacks religious and moral sensibility. This term is used three times in Proverbs. Imagine naming a baby Nabal and condemning him to wear that term all his life (see 1 Samuel 25:2ff.)!

So, who are the stupid people in the book of Proverbs? Try to give the meaning of each of the five terms in two or three words each; say them aloud. Can you begin to see such a person moving around in the life about you?

Now, the Smart People

Being "wise" is the opposite of being a "fool." But what does the word "wisdom" mean, mentioned so often in our book (fifty times in the RSV)?

Much study has been done in recent decades on what is called the "wisdom movement" in Hebrew life. It is now agreed that there were sages, instructors, and groups of teachers not only in Israel but also throughout the Near East. Thus three—not two—groups were very influential in shaping Israel's life: (1) priests, (2) prophets, and (3) wise men, sages, instructors. These last were deeply involved in training both youth (1:8; 2:1; 3:1; etc.) and adults (1:5, 6) in the intelligent, moral life with skills in living in tune with the moral order.

So, the wise person would be *the practical, intelligent, sensible human being who has sound moral standards.*

TO MAKE IT VIVID,

wisdom is personified. A real, live, very attractive Lady Wisdom is pictured as standing in the city square or out on the hills, shouting to all passersby to follow her teaching. Read 8:1-12 and try to see her in your mind's eye; hear her voice rise and fall. Then, look over there at her unworthy counterpart, Dame Stupidity! Read 9:1-5, 13-18, and visualize what is going on.

But the Book of Proverbs Goes One Step Further

Proverbs 1:7 goes further. Read aloud these translations:

"The fear of the Lord is the beginning of knowledge," which is an integral part of wisdom (KJV).

"To have knowledge, you must first have reverence for the LORD."

"How does a man become wise? The first step is to trust and reverence the Lord!" *(The Living Bible)* (The Hebrew lacks a word for "trust" here.)

"The first principle of knowledge is to hold the Lord in awe" *(Anchor Bible).*

We shall not go into detail here on the "fear of the Lord," since chapter 12 is entirely devoted to it, but we must remember that the kind of wisdom talked about in the book of Proverbs is not just maxims about how to handle yourself in relation to other people. It includes a deep reverence for God and a life in accord with that reverence. As a Jewish commentator writes,

> . . . there is one underlying idea which runs like a thread through the thirty-one chapters. Wisdom, we are told again and again, is rooted in God, and foolishness is kin to wickedness. Therefore, wisdom and folly relate to divine justice; He rewards the good, He punishes the wicked. To

Proverbs, this is incontestable, even obvious. . . . (See 3:19; 8:22-36.)[2]

Who Do You Feel Are the Smart People?

In the light of all that has been said in this chapter, who do YOU think are the smart people in today's world?

Imagine that it is the year A.D. 2000. Writers everywhere are asking who, in the twentieth century, were the "smartest" (in this deep sense), the greatest, the people with the most practical integrity? (You can think quickly of several who would NOT be considered.) But who might qualify? Albert Schweitzer? Dag Hammerskjöld? Martin Luther King, Jr.? Eleanor Roosevelt? Pope John XXIII? Mohandas Karamchand Gandhi? Or who? Somehow the present writer feels that in the future there may be some different judgments from those made at the present moment. What do you think?

We cannot leave without asking, "What did our Lord say?"

"So then, anyone who hears these words of mine and obeys them is like a wise man who built his house on rock. [Watch him doing it, in imagination.] The rain poured down, the rivers flooded over, and the wind blew hard against that house [hear the rain beating and the wind whistling]. But it did not fall, because it was built on rock.

"But anyone who hears these words of mine and does not obey them is like a foolish man who built his house on sand. [Watch him.] The rain poured down, the rivers flooded over, the wind blew hard against that house, and it fell [see it sway and then crash]" (Matthew 7:24-27).

Now we know who are the smart and who are the stupid.

What Some Others Have Said

"You can generally get success if you do not want victory."—William Ralphe Inge, *More Lay Thoughts of a Dean*, 1931.

"Life does not require us to make good; it asks only that we give our best at each new level of experience."—Harold W. Ruopp, 1899–1961.

"The secret of success is constancy to purpose."—Benjamin Disraeli, speech, June 24, 1870.

"A failure is a man who has blundered, but is not able to cash in [on] the experience."—Elbert Hubbard, *One Thousand and One Epigrams*, 1905.

"Not failure, but low aim, is crime."—James Russell Lowell, "For An Autograph," *Complete Poetical Works*, 1897.

[2] W. G. Plaut, *Book of Proverbs* (New York: Union of American Hebrew Congregations, 1961), pp. 11, 12. Used by permission of the publisher, the Union of American Hebrew Congregations.

6

How Do You
Handle Your Money
(What There Is of It)?

NEWS ITEM

Marjorie Jackson, heiress of an Indiana grocery chain fortune and known as an eccentric, was found shot to death in her rambling suburban home in Indianapolis. She had hidden $5,000,000 in various places in the house.

Want more money? Look at some of the books on the subject:
How to Have More Money
How to Make Money Selling the Songs You Write
Instant Millionaires: The Secrets of Overnight Success
How I Turned $1000 into Three Million in Real Estate—In My Spare Time
How to Borrow Your Way to a Great Fortune
How I Made $1,000,000 in Mail Order
How to Win at Poker

Look at This

The book jacket of a book on money raises this question: "What is the best way and the quickest way to become wealthy?" What about it? Think for two minutes about whether you really want to be wealthy. If so, how wealthy?

Now let's look at a letter that came recently to the director of a retirement center:

"My income is too low to take care of the expenses of rent, lights, heat, gas, and water, and there is not enough money for food. I do not have any friends, and it is very lonely here. I never go out. I am home all the time. And I would like to be around people. I have sold about everything I had, so I wouldn't have to go on relief. But there is nothing more to sell, so I hope some day you will have a place for me."

LET'S DIVIDE
the following pages into three parts:
Money in the book of Proverbs,
Money in the rest of the Old Testament,
Money in the New Testament.

Money in the Book of Proverbs

We are not surprised that, in a book of down-to-earth advice on how to live, there are many references to money. In fact, there are at least seventy-eight! Let's see what they say.

10:2—Money gotten dishonestly.

10:4—Hard work will make you rich.

10:15—Wealth protects.

10:22—God's blessing makes a man financially rich.

11:3b—The dishonest are destroyed by their dishonesty.

11:4—Wealth not helpful when you die.

11:7—How much confidence do we put in money?

11:16d—The aggressive one will get rich.

11:24—Using money freely and getting richer.

11:25—If you are generous, you'll be prosperous.

11:26—Corner on the grain market!

11:28—Same idea as 11:7, plus a bonus promise for the righteous.

13:7— "Some people pretend to be rich, but have nothing. Others pretend to be poor, but own a fortune."

13:8—Is this verse talking about ransom money?

13:11—The more easily you get it, the sooner you'll lose it.

13:22—Having something to leave to your descendants.

14:20—Is it always true that no one likes a poor man? The rest of the verse certainly "tells it like it is."

14:21—Where kindness comes in.

14:23—"Work and you will earn a living; if you sit around talking, you will be poor."

14:24—The wise will get wealthy.

15:6—"Righteous men keep their wealth, but wicked men lose theirs when hard times come."

15:27a—What if the profit is a bit dishonest?

16:8—"It is better to have a little, honestly earned, than to have a large income, dishonestly gained."

16:16—*Are* wisdom and knowledge preferable to money?

16:19—Loot.

17:5—Making fun of the poor.

17:8—Using money for a bribe. (See chapter 8 of this book.)

17:16—It's no good trying to educate a fool.

17:18—Being responsible for a neighbor's debt.

17:28—If he keeps his mouth shut.

18:11—How much protection?

18:23—While the poor beg, *are* the rich rude, always? Most of the time? Never?

19:1—Poor but honest.

19:4—The rich always have friends; how about the poor?

19:7—The poor man's brothers.

19:17—Giving to the poor is lending to God.

19:22—"It is a disgrace to be greedy."

20:10 Dishonest weights.

20:15— Better than money.

20:17—"What you get by dishonesty you may enjoy like the finest food, but sooner or later it will be like a mouthful of sand."

20:21—The more easily money comes, the less good it will do.

20:23—See 20:10.

21:5—If you plan, you'll have plenty.

21:6—Raise questions, talk back, discuss this one.

21:13—When we refuse the cry of the poor, we. . . .

21:17—Luxuries, etc.

21:20—Wise men live in wealth and luxury.

21:26a—Just thinking about it. . . .

21:26b—Who can give generously?

22:1—Which: a good reputation, or a fat pocketbook?

22:2—God makes the rich and the poor.

22:4—God-fearers get rich.

22:7—The poor are the slaves of the rich.

22:9—Be generous!

22:16— How to become poor.

22:22—Don't take advantage of poor people!

22:26, 27—Being responsible for other people's debts.

23:4—On wearing yourself out making money.

23:5—Your money can go like a flash!

24:15—Don't rob.

24:27—Building a house before you can afford it?

25:12—"A warning given by an experienced person to someone willing to listen is more valuable than gold rings. . . ."

27:23-27—Wealth doesn't last forever, so. . . .

28:3—How do you treat the poor?

28:6—Poor and honest.

28:8—Now about interest.

28:11—Rich people think they're wise.

28:15—Are the poor helpless?

28:19b—How to be poor.

28:20, 22—What if you're in a hurry to get rich?

28:24—On stealing from your parents.

28:27—"Give to the poor and you will never be in need."

29:3b—Spending money on prostitutes

29:4—When the king is too concerned with money.

29:13—Does this mean that God permits both poverty and oppression of the poor?

30:7-9—A prayer about money.

30:14—How NOT to make a living! But some do.

31:3b—Advice for the king about money.

QUESTIONS, QUESTIONS

If you don't have a lot of questions about these, you didn't look them up! Questions like

How can I be sure that if I give to the poor I'll never be in need myself (28:27)?

If I plan, WILL I really have plenty (21:5)?

(Take time to formulate six or seven more questions.)

WE MUST REMEMBER

that the book of Proverbs represents the thinking of the educated and the comparatively well-off class. It was a leisure group which usually inherited money and then passed it on to the next generation. The temptation was strong to look down on the poor (19:4, 7)! It looks as if the poor-rich rift has been around for a long time!

Money in the Rest of the Old Testament

However, in the Old Testament there is the strong belief that everything belongs to God (Psalm 24:1). God "lets out" his bounty to his people, but ". . . you must never think that you have made yourselves wealthy by your own power and strength" (Deuteronomy 8:17). So God gives prosperity to those who obey him. And when men become greedy, cheaters, seeking wealth for the sake of wealth, they pay very stiff penalties (see the book of Amos).

The book of Proverbs has a healthy reminder for us that material resources are really necessary to support good causes. As Rylaarsdam says, ". . . it is dangerous to speak as though goodness could exist apart from power, either in God or man."[1]

nevertheless

God has a special place in his heart for the poor. He made them (22:2). The book of Deuteronomy contains scores of laws reflecting a kindly concern for those without material advantages. And so, too, in Proverbs being poor is much preferable to being a fool (19:1) or a liar (19:22). And "If you refuse to listen to the cry of the poor, your own cry for help will not be heard" (21:13).

What About the New Testament?

Jesus was pessimistic about a rich man's being able to escape from subservience to his money (Luke 12:16ff.). But ". . . a person's true life is not made up of the things he owns, no matter how rich he may be" (Luke 12:15). "You cannot serve both God and money" (Matthew 6:24d).

The concern for the poor runs throughout the New Testament, resulting, for a short time, in a community which held all property jointly (Acts 4:32-35). And Paul urges giving to those less fortunate (2 Corinthians 8:13-15).

How Do You Spend Your Money?

There are plenty of secular books telling us how to plan the budget. Write down three principles that guide *you* in the spending of *your* money:

1. _____

_____

[1] J. C. Rylaarsdam, *The Proverbs, Ecclesiastes, The Song of Solomon,* The Layman's Bible Commentary, vol. 10 (Richmond, Virginia: John Knox Press, 1964), p. 69. © M. E. Bratcher 1964. Used by permission of John Knox Press.

2. _____

_____

3. _____

_____

We can do no better than to end with an imaginary bill if God should suddenly decide to send us a monthly statement. Would it run something like this?

Due to God for services rendered during one month:

30 days of care and supervision, air, light, sunlight, and rain;

240 hours of restful, re-creative sleep;

720 hours of physical upkeep of heart, lungs, senses, digestion, locomotion;

90 very satisfying meals;

1 competent mind to analyze and judge, a memory to retain, a will to act;

A family that loves you, rejoices, and sorrows with you;

A host of friends who believe in you and overlook your oddities and mistakes;

Neighbors, near and far, who band together to build a better community;

Skies and seasons that bring beauty and grandeur, parks, and gardens;

A church that is free and strong, affording you worship, guidance, friendship, and love;

Love from a God of justice, compassion, and forgiveness, whose plans and purposes were spelled out by his Son, and whose Spirit abides in you.[2]

In the light of this, how DO we spend our money?

What Some Others Have Said

"Get to know two things about an individual, how he makes his money and how he spends it, and you have the 'open sesame' to his character. You have a searchlight that will show up the inmost recesses of his soul. You know all you need to know about his desires, his values, his standards, his religion."—Robert James McCracken, "The Stub of an Old Checkbook," a sermon delivered in Riverside Church, New York City, Nov. 3, 1957. Used by permission.

[2] Author unknown.

"He that gets money before he gets wit,
Will be but a short while master of it."
—Thomas Fuller, *Gnomologia,* 1732.

"The moral flabbiness born of the exclusive worship of . . . SUC-CESS. That—with the squalid cash interpretation put on the word success— is our national disease."—William James, letter to H. G Wells, Sept. 11, 1906.

"Money is a good servant, but a bad master."—Anonymous.

"He that is of the opinion Money will do every Thing, may well be suspected of doing every Thing for Money."—Benjamin Franklin, *Poor Richard's Almanack,* July, 1753.

"This will never be a civilized country until we expend more money for books than we do for chewing gum."—Elbert Hubbard, *The Philistine,* vol. 25, 1913.

7
The Company We Keep

The following letters were received not very long ago by a prominent minister:
"I'm all mixed up and I know it. I am a senior in high school and run with a gang. We have tried everything, and I mean everything . . . I don't want to live like this."[1]

and

"I grew up in a Christian home, but a few years ago I began chasing around with the gang, and did things I'm ashamed of."[2]

Make a Guess

Do you think the above letters were written by young, middle-aged, or older people? By males or females? Whites or Blacks? Americans or non-Americans? THEY MIGHT HAVE BEEN WRITTEN BY ANYBODY, ANYTIME, REPRESENTING ANY NATIONAL GROUP.

A seventeenth-century writer put it, "A man is known by the company he keeps." How far is this true? Completely? Partially?

Read that quotation aloud. If the reader is not a man, change it to "A woman is known by the company she keeps." Now change it once more and read aloud, "I am known by the company I keep."

Does the Book of Proverbs Help Here?

There are at least sixteen passages which relate to this subject:

1:10-19

2:11-15

[1] Billy Graham, *My Answer* (New York: Doubleday & Co., Inc., 1960), p. 71.
[2] *Ibid.,* p. 118.

2:16-19
4:14
6:24, 25
9:6
13:20
14:7
16:29
16:30
22:14
22:24, 25
23:20
24:1, 2
25:17
28:7

Read these passages; at once you see that they describe the people who are NOT recommended as companions; they are the ones to stay away from. You see the truth of the following: ". . . negative commands are a favorite—though not exclusive—method of Jewish moral teaching."[3]

It will be worth your while to fill in these sixteen spaces, naming very specifically the kinds of companions who are warned against:

1. (e.g., racketeers) _____

2. _____

3. _____

4. _____

5. _____

6. _____

7. _____

8. _____

9. _____

10. _____

[3] W. G. Plaut, *Book of Proverbs, A Commentary* (New York: Union of American Hebrew Congregations, 1961), p. 34. Used by permission of the publisher, the Union of American Hebrew Congregations.

11. _____

12. _____

13. _____

14. _____

15. _____

16. _____

(If you find that some of these are hard to boil down to a few vivid words, try different translations.)

Questions

Now, so you won't say, "Well, these warnings don't really apply to me and my family," let's raise some questions that quickly come to mind as one reads the passages thoughtfully:

✓ Why do boys and girls from good homes sometimes join tough groups and eventually end up as criminals (1:10-19)?

✓ Why is there an underworld of gangsters? Why are there other kinds of violent persons?

✓ How does the first murder affect a killer?

✓ Why is there so much ruthless cruelty in the world?

✓ How does callousness to the value of life ever begin? Does war have something to do with it? How much?

✓ What do you think of this statement: "Two great dangers confront every youth: wrong associates and loose women"?[4] Only youth?

✓ Do we all have times when wrong begins to seem right, and right wrong? This is what we call the upside-down world of values. The word in 2:12 translated "perverted" (RSV) comes from a Hebrew verb meaning "turn upside down."

✓ How about this: "Proverbs retains the optimistic view that reason and will, properly trained and disciplined, can overcome the hazards in the human situation"?[5] Do you believe this?

✓ Does this Rabbinic maxim furnish a clue to the matter of friendships and companionships: "Let thy house be a meeting place

---

[4] Plaut, *op. cit.,* p. 47.

[5] J. C. Rylaarsdam, *The Proverbs, Ecclesiastes, The Song of Solomon;* The Layman's Bible Commentary (Richmond, Virginia: John Knox Press, 1964), vol. 10, pp. 56, 57. © M. E. Bratcher, 1964. Used by permission of John Knox Press.

for the wise . . ."?[6] How far can this be carried out today?

Is it true that "the regeneration of a fool is so highly improbable [in Proverbs] that it is not worth any risks"?[7] Proverbs 14:7 seems to imply this.

✓ How do you feel about crime stories on TV? Do they, or don't they, leave the impression that crime does not pay?

✓ Are there hopeless criminals around us who are at large? What is the solution to this problem?

✓ Is our age sex-obsessed?

✓ Does the crowd at sporting events like professional football and hockey come hoping for "blood," fights, and violence?

✓ In the matter of "chumminess" with neighbors (25:17), how do we avoid "wearing out our welcome"?

Now Ask, "Why Are Your Best Friends Your Best Friends?"

Make a study of a cluster of close friends (use your own "set," preferably.) Ask these questions:

How did the friendships begin? How long have they lasted? Have there been breaks in their continuity?

What bonds have helped the group to stay together?

What do the friends like best to do together?

Have there been forces tending to break the group apart?

Is there a mild age variation in the set, or a considerable one?

Does the group include both sexes?

Would you characterize it as an "evening set," "business friends," "weekend group," or what?

Write three sentences below on "The Influence of Three Close Friends on My Life."

_____

_____

_____

What are you most proud of as you remember these relationships? Least proud of?

Finally, Some Positive Suggestions

First, the book of Proverbs *assumes that we can pick our*

[6] *Mishna, Aboth,* 1.4.
[7] Rylaarsdam, *op. cit.,* p. 57.

companions. Most of us can pick at least the closest ones.

In Proverbs 1:20-33 and in chapters 8 and 9, wisdom, which has been described as meaning, in different contexts, such things as skill in living, good sense, and moral understanding, is personified: Lady Wisdom is always shouting to the crowd to live the sensible, thought-out life. Dame Stupidity, on the other hand, is equally vociferous in tempting people to do the exact opposite. BUT THE CHOICE HAS TO BE MADE!

Another way of putting it is found in Proverbs 3:1-10 and in chapter 4. The term "my son" does double duty: here is the father giving instruction to his own boy at home (see chapter 4); it is also the teacher facing his class and giving instruction for living (see 22:17ff.). And what is more, many of the maxims are given here for ADULT consumption (see 1:2-6). It's SO easy for us to apply the book only to youth; BUT IT APPLIES TO ALL OF US! Choices come to every one of us daily, and we are the ones who select the companions who make or break us!

There are two corollaries here:

1. Don't get drafted into a "set." YOU must do the choosing.
2. And don't *drift* into one, either.

Some time ago a businessman was approached by his associates. "We've got something good, and we want to cut you in." What was it? An apartment with attractive girls on call had been rented by the group. It was used daily. The men went home at night as usual to their families. "We want to cut you in." The businessman went along. But he had strong church relationships. And finally the crisis came—and, thank God, it was resolved in the right way.

E. W. Scripps, the founder of the Scripps-Howard chain of newspapers, was asked once why he spent so much time on his Western ranch. His reply:

> "I'm a rich man, and that's dangerous, you know. But it isn't the money that's the risk, it's the living around other rich men. They get to thinking all alike; and their money not only talks, their money does their thinking, too. I come off here on these wide acres of high miles to get away from my sort." [8]

Or, as a fifteenth-century proverb has put it, "Better be alone than in bad company."

Finally, if you and I are known by the company we keep, then there

[8] G. B. Oxnam, *Preaching in a Revolutionary Age* (Nashville: Abingdon-Cokesbury Press, 1944), p. 174.

is one more word: there is for the Christian the CREATIVE COMPANIONSHIP OF CHRIST ("You are my friends . . . I call you friends . . ." John 15:14a, 15b) and also THE CLOUD OF UNSEEN WITNESSES (see Hebrews 12:1, RSV).

"Beside us walks our brother Christ
And makes our task his own."[9]

What Some Others Have Said

"He that goeth to bed with dogs ariseth with fleas."—James Sandford, *Houres of Recreation,* 1576.

"If a man can be known by nothing else, then he may be known by his companions."—Henry Smith, *Preparative to Mariage,* 1591.

"What men call . . . good fellowship, is commonly but the virtue of pigs in a litter which lie close together to keep each other warm."—Henry David Thoreau, *Journal,* Oct. 23, 1852.

"Who keeps company with the wolf learns to howl."—Thomas Fuller, *Gnomologia,* 1732.

"The wise man will want to be ever with him who is better than himself."—Plato, *Phaedo.*

"Lay aside the best book whenever you can go into the best company; and depend on it, you change for the better."—Lord Chesterfield, *Letters,* 1752.

"To be everybody's friend is to be nobody's friend. For friendship is the feeling you possess for a particular person as distinct from all other persons. It is a very beautiful and intimate and close relationship which is destroyed if it is bestowed casually."—Attributed to St. John Ervine, 1883–1971.

[9] Ozora S. Davis, hymn, "We Bear the Strain of Earthly Care."

8

What's Wrong with a Little Gift to Help Things Along? Do You Have to Call It a Bribe?

Well, if this isn't a timely subject! Here are the opening words of the titles of some recent magazine articles:

"Bribery: a Shocker"   "Is Bribery Defensible?"
"Everybody's Doing It?"   "Senate Action Expected"
"Kickback Scourge"   "Fallout of Bribery"
"Winks and Roars"   "Ethics Not Customs"
"Unscandalized Views"   "Warning Quagmire Ahead"

A Definition

Exactly WHAT is a bribe? The unabridged dictionary defines it as "a price, reward, gift, or favor bestowed or promised with a view to pervert the judgment or corrupt the conduct especially of a person in a position of trust (as a public official)."

Any Relevant Proverbs?

Yes, of course. Bribery wasn't invented last year.

15:27b—Don't take bribes and you will live longer."

17:8—"Some people think a bribe works like magic; they believe it can do anything."

17:23—"Corrupt judges accept secret bribes, and then justice is not done."

18:16—"Do you want to meet an important person? Take him a gift and it will be easy."

21:14—"If someone is angry with you, a gift given secretly will calm him down."

65

28:21—"Prejudice is wrong. But some judges will do wrong to get even the smallest bribe."

29:4 "When the king is concerned with justice, the nation will be strong, but when he is only concerned with money, he will ruin his country."

Any Explanations Needed?

Yes. What do you think of 15:27b? What does it mean when it says that one who turns down bribery will live longer? Look at these other translations:

King James Version: ". . . shall live."

New American Standard Bible and RSV: ". . . will live."

The Living Bible: " . . hating bribes brings happiness."

Jerusalem Bible: ". . . shall have life."

New English Bible: ". . . will enjoy long life."

Moffatt: ". . . shall prosper."

Scott in Anchor Bible: ". . . will live [in peace]."

(The first two are literal renderings of the Hebrew.)

Without reading more in here than the author meant, we can probably conclude that he is saying, "A person who cannot be bribed has an enviable quality of life."

But 17:8 is anything but easy. Ten of the translations I consulted say "bribe"; two have the neutral term "gift." Note the following translations:

"A gift works like a talisman for him who gives it: he prospers whichever way he turns" (Jerusalem Bible).

"A gift is a lucky stone in the eyes of him who receives it, Wherever he turns, he will prosper" (Anchor Bible). But in a note there is an alternate translation: "A bribe is like a charm in the eyes of the giver." One problem is that the Hebrew word sometimes means "bribe" and sometimes just plain "gift." So the translations vary. The New American Bible is helpful at this point: "A man who has a bribe to offer rates it a magic stone; at every turn it brings him success." But the RSV is more literal: "A bribe is like a magic stone in the eyes of him who gives it; wherever he turns he prospers." At any rate we must avoid the rendering in The Living Bible, "A bribe works like magic. Whoever uses it will prosper!" even with the qualifying footnote, for the Hebrew says literally, "A bribe . . . in the eyes of its owner. . . ." The verse is, to say the least, a tribute to the potency of a bribe; but that does not justify bribery.

17:23 is just as clear as 17:8 is difficult. *The Living Bible* is brief and powerful: "It is wrong to accept a bribe to twist justice."

We shall dismiss 18:16 because most feel that the reference is to an innocent gift.

That leaves three other passages. 21:14 says literally, as in RSV, "A gift in secret averts anger; and a bribe in the bosom, strong wrath." And if the first clause doesn't refer to a bribe (yet why is the gift secret?), the second half does. *Jerusalem Bible* is clear: "Anger is mollified by a covert gift, raging fury by a bribe under cover of the cloak."

If with Scott we take the reference 28:21 to mean a court judge's tipping the scales because of certain considerations (!), then the second clause may refer to the very small bribe demanded by some, or it may urge clemency toward one who breaks the law because of need, without any reference to the first clause. Scott renders it: "To show partiality [in a judicial decision] is wrong; a man may be at fault [even] over a morsel of food" *(Anchor Bible)*.

And the last reference, 29:4, refers either to a king who weakens his country by extortion, or one who demands bribes. The *New American Standard Bible* takes it in the second sense: "The king gives stability to the land by justice, But a man who takes bribes overthrows it" (a good example of "corruption in high places").

Bribery in the Proverbs, then, especially evident in judicial procedure, is heavily frowned upon, just as it is expressly forbidden in the Law (Deuteronomy 16:19; see also 1 Samuel 8:3; Job 15:34). And it is only those who consistently refuse to "take a bribe against the innocent" who can dwell in the presence of God (Psalm 15:5, RSV). As Rylaarsdam writes, "The almost exclusively evil meaning of bribery associated with 'gifts' from one public figure to another in Israelite society corresponds closely to the suspicion with which the public views 'gifts' sometimes made to public officials by representatives of industry today."[1]

Now, What Is Being Said Today?
Comments and Questions in the 1970s

Turn back to the list of current articles in our periodicals; the list might have been multiplied by twenty. As one of them says, "Scandals involving money, misuse of power and, occasionally,

[1] J. C. Rylaarsdam, *The Proverbs, Ecclesiastes, The Song of Solomon*, The Layman's Bible Commentary, vol. 10 (Richmond, Va.: John Knox Press, 1964), p. 64. © M. E. Bratcher 1964. Used by permission of John Knox Press.

sexual misconduct have been in the headlines for years. Since the end of World War II, more than 50 incidents have captured the public's interest." [2]

But is this something new? Our history books (the honest ones) tell us that graft was commonplace in the American colonies. And the financing of the American Revolution was solidly based on conflicts of interest wholeheartedly welcomed by a government that was just about penniless. Then Alexander Hamilton is recorded as having used graft "from a sense of duty." And the president of the Second Bank of the United States gave Daniel Webster a check for $10,000 after he made a speech in the Senate in favor of the bank.

But the "golden age" of graft followed the Civil War. Jay Gould, who may well have owned (by manipulations) about 10 percent of all the U.S. railroad track in 1880, once went to the state capital in Albany, New York, with a valise containing half a million dollars and returned with it empty. And tycoon Collis P. Huntington in 1877 wrote to a friend, "If you have to pay money to have the right thing done, it is only just and fair to do it."

But by the early years of the twentieth century a wave of public concern over business ethics was beginning to roll in. Yet in spite of some reform legislation, Secretary of the Interior Albert B. Fall accepted bribes from oilmen and served time in prison in the Teapot Dome scandal. [3]

And in recent months we have watched scandal after scandal rising like an ominous specter—scandals involving over two hundred great corporations, many highly respected. In self-defense, a former chairman of the Lockheed Corporation said, "I am not arguing that it is a good practice . . . I am saying unless everybody plays by the same rules, if you are going to win, it is necessary." Some others have argued that to do business abroad, the moral standards current in other countries must be adopted.

Now, What Do You Say?

Let's get a little closer to home. Ask yourself some of these questions:

When does a gift become a bribe?

---

[2] *U. S. News & World Report,* Aug. 1, 1977, p. 12.

[3] I owe much of the preceding information to the article by John Brooks, "The Businessman and the Government: Corruption, Yesterday and Today," *American Heritage,* vol. 28, no. 4, June, 1977.

Is there anything wrong with gifts of appreciation?

You are in an overseas country, going through customs which can be a time-consuming ordeal. A "middleman" who knows the "ropes" (and the people) is helping you and saving you no end of time. You pay him a fee beyond the customs figure (or perhaps beyond a nominal customs figure), and he takes your papers through the various offices with favored treatment. By distributing part of his fee in different offices, he saves you a lot of time. Is this bribery?

How many companies do you know that give liquor or other presents to valued customers at Christmas time? What about this? Gifts of appreciation?

Do you know that the New Testament does not mention bribes? (But you can certainly find references to unjust judges!)

NOW WRITE DOWN HERE 1, 2, OR 3 CONCLUSIONS at which you have arrived:

_____

_____

_____

_____

As these lines are being written, there is great discussion about codes of ethics for people in public life. Is it possible that in our country there is an equally desperate need of a new code of ethics for those of us in *private* life?

The world, if it is to be a better place in which to live, must have better nations. But nations are made up of individuals. And if individuals are going to improve, that's getting down to people like you and me. In fact, it gets RIGHT DOWN to YOU and ME.

What Some Others Have Said

"Yang Tsen, a mandarin of the Han dynasty, was brought a bribe in the night and assured that no one would know. He replied, 'Heaven knows, Earth knows, you know, and I know.' *(T'ien chih, ti chih, ni chih, wo chih.)"*—W. Scarborough, *A Collection of Chinese Proverbs,* 1875.

"There is nothing I detest so much as a crooked politician or corrupt government official. But the type of businessman who is a fixer is even lower in my estimation."—Harry S. Truman, *Mr. President,* 1952.

"Bribes will enter without knocking."—John Ray, *English Proverbs,* 1670.

"Corruption never has been compulsory."—Anthony Eden.

"Take no bribe, surrender no right."—Cervantes, *Don Quixote,* 1615.

"Bribery and theft are first cousins."—Anonymous.

"It is perilous to buy from a few what belongs to the many."—Sallust, *Bellum Iugurthinum, ca.* 40 B.C.

"Teach me that 60 minutes make an hour, 16 ounces a pound, and 100 cents a dollar. Help me to live so that I can lie down at night with a clear conscience and unhaunted by the faces of those to whom I may have brought pain. Grant that I may earn my meal ticket on the square, and in earning it I may do unto others as I would have them do unto me. Deafen me to the tingle of tainted money."—Author unknown.

9

When Old Age Comes On

> *"I believe that old age is a gift, a very precious gift, not a calamity."*
> *"Since it is a gift, I thank God for it daily."*[1]

BUT

this is NOT the popular view. So now we print, UPSIDE DOWN ON PURPOSE (since they are WRONG), some stereotyped pictures of the elderly:

"Once you are old you are 'fading fast,' 'over the hill,' 'out to pasture,' 'down the drain,' 'finished,' 'out-of-date,' an 'old crock,' 'fogy,' 'geezer,' or 'biddy,'"[2]

1. Most old people live in institutions.
2. Most old people are constantly in bed because of illness.
3. After sixty-five everyone goes steadily downhill.
4. Old people are typically alone, abandoned by family and lonely.
5. People should retire; older people can't do a decent job.
6. Everyone knows old folks are past having sex.
7. After sixty-five your mind deteriorates and you can expect to get senile.
8. Old folks spend all their time sitting around watching television.
9. Disengagement is a natural acceptance of old-age limitations—older people really welcome it.
10. Most of the handicaps of older people are physical; after all, they are old.[3]

[1] John La Farge, *Reflections on Growing Old* (New York: Doubleday & Company, Inc., 1963), p. 13.

[2] Robert N. Butler, *Why Survive? Being Old in America* (New York: Harper & Row, Publishers, 1975), pp. 1, 2.

[3] Alex Comfort, *A Good Age* (New York: Crown Publishers, Inc., 1976), pp. 86-89. © Mitchell Beagley Publishers Limited 1976. Used by permission of Crown Publishers, Inc.

Any Word for It in Proverbs?

Interestingly enough, we find only four references to this subject in the book of Proverbs (unless I missed some, which is quite possible):

3:17 is only a general reference: "Wisdom can make your life pleasant and lead you safely through it."

5:10 and 11 remind us grimly about the man who has "gone off the deep end" in adultery.

16:31: "Long life is the reward of the righteous; gray hair is a glorious crown."

And 20:29: "We admire the strength of youth and respect the gray hair of age."

THE FIRST THING

we notice is that *almost all* of our questions about aging aren't even mentioned here! Questions like

✓ How can we prepare for old age?

✓ Will we be eccentric?

✓ How can I possibly support myself in old age?

✓ Should old people live with their children?

✓ Is it advisable to marry after sixty-five?

✓ Who really believes that "the best is yet to be"?

✓ What are the sources of assistance to which I can turn?

✓ What diseases should I fear most?

What About the Rest of the Old Testament?

The interesting regulations in Leviticus 27:1-7 place the age of sixty as the dividing line between full usefulness and old age. Yet respect for age was very characteristic of Hebrew life; Leviticus 19:32a says "Show respect for old people and honor them." Honoring of fathers and mothers is one of the basic commandments (Exodus 20:12). And take time to read Ruth 4:15. It is only in a chaotic society that "young people will not respect their elders" (Isaiah 3:5b). Long life is promised for obedience to God (Deuteronomy 30:20). And if you want to see an amazing picture of ages at the new creation, turn to Isaiah 65:20. And if you are ready for it, or up to it, read Ecclesiastes 12:1-7 (with the help of a commentary to help you identify the references to parts of the body) for a classic description of what old age can do to us!

Some, but not all, of the old men achieved the position of "elder" in the community, but this is a subject in itself.

And the New Testament?

1 Timothy 5:1, 2 reads, "Do not rebuke an older man, but appeal to him as if he were your father. Treat the younger men as your brothers, the older women as mothers, and the younger women as sisters, with all purity."

Would You Help?

You can write this next section as well as anybody else. Yes, it's been written up in the books on aging (tons of them), but you can do it; please spend fifteen minutes in writing down TEN SUGGESTIONS FOR OLDER PEOPLE BY WHICH THEY CAN WIN THE RESPECT OF THOSE WHO ARE YOUNGER.

1. For example, to start it off, we'll quote: "React to people who talk slightingly about seniors ('old duffer,' 'old biddy,' 'dirty old man,' 'old lady in tennis shoes'). Tell them you don't appreciate that sort of language. . . . Usually they mean no harm, but need their heads changed to see older people as people. . . ."[4]

2. _____

_____

3. _____

_____

4. _____

_____

5. _____

_____

6. _____

_____

7. _____

_____

8. _____

_____

---

[4] Comfort, *op. cit.,* p. 63.

9. _____

_____

10. _____

_____

Would the Following Facts Encourage You?

"Grandma" Moses began to paint in oils at the age of 78.

When P. G. Wodehouse died at 93 he had written over a hundred books and was at work on another.

Thomas A. Edison took out a patent on the last of his 1,033 inventions when he was 81.

Fred Streeter, BBC's famous gardening expert, broadcasted only a few hours before his death at the age of 98.

Charlie Smith, officially recognized as the oldest United States resident in 1972 at the age of 120, was made to quit his citrus farm at the age of 113 because he was judged too old to climb trees.

Franz Liszt, Hungarian concert pianist, toured Europe giving brilliant recitals when he was 74.

Artur Rubenstein will long be remembered for his remarkable piano recital in Carnegie Hall when he was 89.

George Bernard Shaw produced his last play when he was in his late 80s.[5]

Let's wind up this study with the oft-quoted prayer which was written by a nun:

> Lord, Thou knowest better than I know myself that I am growing older, and will someday be old.
>
> Keep me from getting talkative, and particularly from the fatal habit of thinking I must say something on every subject and on every occasion.
>
> Release me from craving to try to straighten out everybody's affairs.
>
> Keep my mind free from the recital of endless details. Give me wings to get to the point.
>
> I ask for grace enough to listen to the tales of others' pains. Help me endure them with patience.
>
> But seal my lips on my own aches and pains. They are increasing and my love of rehearsing them is becoming sweeter as the years go by.
>
> Teach me the glorious lesson that occasionally it is possible that I may be mistaken.

[5] I owe the above information to Alex Comfort's *A Good Age, op. cit.* His book contains excellent line drawings of these people and others. The present writer would disagree with one or two ethical judgments in the book, but found it immensely helpful.

Keep me reasonably sweet. I do not want to be a saint—some of them are so hard to live with—but a sour old woman is one of the crowning works of the devil.

Make me thoughtful, but not moody; helpful, but not bossy. With my vast store of wisdom, it seems a pity not to use it all—but Thou knowest, Lord, that I want a few friends at the end![6]

So, about whom have we been talking? "An 'aged' person is simply a person who has been there longer than a young person."[7]

What Some Others Have Said

"We get too soon old, and too late smart."—Anonymous.

"We are always the same age inside."—Gertrude Stein (1874–1946), as quoted in Franklin Pierce Adams, *FPA Book of Quotations*, 1952.

"Some are old at 20; their notions harden long before their arteries do."—Attributed to E. B. White (1899–   ).

"In the days of my youth I remembered my God, And He hath not forgotten my age."—Robert Southey, *The Old Man's Comforts*, 1797.

"To me, fair friend, you never can be old"—Shakespeare, *Sonnets*, CIV.

"To be seventy years young is sometimes far more cheerful and hopeful than to be forty years old."—Author unknown.

> "As a white candle
> In a holy place,
> So is the beauty
> Of an aged face."

—Joseph Campbell (also Seosamh MacCathmhaoil), *The Old Woman*, 1920. Used by permission of S. Campbell, executor of the estate.

---

[6] This prayer, written by a Roman Catholic nun, has had several published appearances.

[7] Comfort, *op. cit.*, p. 28.

10

Do We Eat and Drink Too Much?

DO WE EAT TOO MUCH?

News Item

The fattest man who ever lived was Robert E. Hughes of Monticello, Illinois, who, according to the record books, tipped the scales at 1041 pounds when he died in 1958 at the age of 32.

DO WE DRINK TOO MUCH?

Magazine Article

Adlai Stevenson wrote in 1959, "No society has ever spent so much as we do on drink and tranquilizers."[1]

The first thing to say on the subject of eating and drinking is that we certainly don't lack books on the subject! Here are some titles:

Eat Yourself Thin
In Praise of Ale
Eat the Weeds
Drinking in College

Eating, Loving, and Dying
Facts and Fantasies About Alcohol
Food Habits
Bread for the World

---

[1] "Politics and Morality," *Saturday Review,* Feb. 7, 1959, p. 13. Quoted in John H. Scammon, *Living with the Psalms* (Valley Forge, Pa.: Judson Press, 1967), p. 98.

I suggest that you make this a DO-IT-YOURSELF chapter. First, we shall ask,

What Does the Book of Proverbs Say About Eating and Drinking?

EATING

13:25—"The righteous have enough to eat, but the wicked are always hungry."

16:24—". . . honey—sweet to the taste and good for your health."

16:26—"A laborer's appetite makes him work harder, because he wants to satisfy his hunger."

17:1—"Better to eat a dry crust of bread with peace of mind than have a banquet in a house full of trouble."

19:24—"Some people are too lazy to put food in their own mouths." (The same as 26:15)

20:13b—"Keep busy and you will have plenty to eat."

20:17—"What you get by dishonesty you may enjoy like the finest food, but sooner or later it will be like a mouthful of sand."

22:9a—"Be generous and share your food with the poor. . . ."

23:1-3—"When you sit down to eat with an important man, keep in mind who he is. If you have a big appetite, restrain yourself. Don't be greedy for the fine food he serves; he may be trying to trick you."

23:6-8—"Don't eat at the table of a stingy man or be greedy for

DRINKING

20:1—"Drinking too much makes you loud and foolish. It's stupid to get drunk."

23:29-35—"Show me someone who drinks too much, who has to try out fancy drinks, and I will show you someone miserable and sorry for himself, always causing trouble and always complaining. His eyes are bloodshot, and he has bruises that could have been avoided. Don't let wine tempt you, even though it is rich red, and it sparkles in the cup, and it goes down smoothly. The next morning you will feel as if you had been bitten by a poisonous snake. Weird sights will appear before your eyes, and you will not be able to think or speak clearly. You will feel as if you were out on the ocean, seasick, swinging high up in the rigging of a tossing ship. 'I must have been hit,' you will say; 'I must have been beaten up, but I don't remember it. Why can't I wake up? I need another drink.'"

31:4b-7—"Kings should not drink wine or have a craving for alcohol. When they drink, they forget the laws and ignore the rights of people in need. Alcohol is for people who are dying,

the fine food he serves. 'Come on and have some more,' he says, but he doesn't mean it. What he thinks is what he really is. You will vomit up what you have eaten, and all your flattery will be wasted."

24:13a—"Son, eat honey; it is good."

25:27a—"Too much honey is bad for you."

27:7—"When you are full, you will refuse honey, but when you are hungry, even bitter food tastes sweet."

27:26-27—"You can make clothes from the wool of your sheep and buy land with the money you get from selling some of your goats. The rest of the goats will provide milk for you and your family, and for your servant girls as well."

28:19—"A hard-working farmer has plenty to eat. People who waste time will always be poor."

30:8b—"So give me only as much food as I need."

for those who are in misery. Let them drink and forget their poverty and unhappiness."

BOTH EATING AND DRINKING

21:17—"Indulging in luxuries, wine, and rich food will never make you wealthy."

23:20-21—"Don't associate with people who drink too much wine or stuff themselves with food. Drunkards and gluttons will be reduced to poverty. If all you do is eat and sleep, you will soon be wearing rags."

25:21-22—"If your enemy is hungry, feed him; if he is thirsty, give him a drink. You will make him burn with shame, and the LORD will reward you."

Raise Questions—Talk Back

Which quotations do you agree with as universally true? Do you feel that there are exceptions as you look at life around you? Are there some that you need to think about? Do you wonder—

1. If it is *always* true that good people have enough to eat? See 13:25.

2. In the light of 20:1, why some, both men and women, drink too much?

3. Whether excessive eating and drinking are a disease?

4. About the first part of 28:19?

5. About 31:6 and quite a number of other passages?

Now, Some Reliable Facts and Figures to Work With

A Few Facts About Eating

1. "Obesity has become in our time a national problem. . . ."[2] Let us not hurry over this statement.

2. "Suppose, as you sat down to your dinner, the doorbell rang. You opened the door, and there before you, ragged and disease-ravaged, stood the world's hungry in a single line, each begging for a crust of bread. How far do you think that line would reach? Beginning at your door, the line would continue out of sight, over continent and ocean, around the world—25,000 miles—and return to the place it started; and it would do this, circling the globe not once, not five times, but twenty-five times, with no one in the line but hungry, suffering humanity."[3]

3. United Nations experts claim that there are about 230,000,000 hungry children at this very moment. Try to visualize their faces. But the experts add that there are at least 350,000,000 other youngsters that have not been reached—580,000,000 in all. This is equivalent to the entire population of North and South America.

4. Light ten candles. Every 8½ seconds, blow one out; during that brief period somebody somewhere in the world has just died of starvation or of some disease related to malnutrition.

---

[2] Jean Mayer, *Overweight, Causes, Cost, and Control* (Englewood Cliffs, N.J.: Prentiss-Hall, 1968), p. 1.

[3] A. Leonard Griffith, "The Age of Shrug," *Deer Park Church Magazine,* Toronto, June, 1971. Used by permission of the author.

5. A group of Methodist ministers in North and South Dakota were invited to a special luncheon. Six percent of those invited were served a full-course meal. But 20 percent of the guests found themselves looking at just soup and bread. The great majority, 70 percent, just received bread. And the remaining 4 percent faced completely empty plates; all they had to eat was what their fellow ministers shared from their lunches. The luncheon represented what today's population gets to eat.

Now, a Few Facts and Figures About Drinking

1. "Drinking alcoholic beverages seems to be an accepted part of life for some groups today. There is a large number of social drinkers who use alcohol in moderation, and there is a large number of people who are problem drinkers—people who either can't stop or don't know when to stop. . . . Yet nationwide it is estimated that about 40 percent of all adults do not drink."[4]

2. In 1976 retail liquor store sales in the U.S. amounted to $11,411,000,000.[5]

3. Alcohol affects different people differently. Yet it is always a depressant, not a stimulant. It is absorbed directly into the bloodstream and quickly affects the brain. First it affects one's judgment and one's inhibitions; if more is drunk, it slows reaction time and coordination; then it affects the vision, speech, and balance. Finally, if heavy drinking continues, the alcohol may produce coma or death.

4. In many states the motor vehicle authorities have ruled that a .10 percent (that is, one-thousandth) content by volume in the bloodstream is evidence of legal intoxication and unfitness for driving.

5. "It is estimated that one out of ten employees in private industry is an alcoholic."[6]

6. "It is now conservatively estimated that there are 8 million cases of alcoholism in this country. . . . At least 20 million husbands, wives,

---

[4]C. G. Wrenn and Shirley Schwarzrock, *Facts and Fantasies About Alcohol,* "Coping With" Series (Circle Pines, Minn.: American Guidance Service, Inc., 1971), pp. 7, 23. This is an excellent series of some twenty-five small paperbacks by two college professors, designed to present facts on a wide range of subjects to young people and then leave them to make decisions.

[5]*The World Almanac & Book of Facts, 1978* (New York: Newspaper Enterprise Association, 1977), p. 103.

[6]Jack B. Weiner, *Drinking* (New York: W. W. Norton & Co., Inc., 1976), p. 7.

and dependent children are directly affected by the alcoholic member of their family."[7]

7. According to the Department of Health, Education, and Welfare, alcoholism cost the nation in 1975 over $42,750,000,000 a year (in loss in work production, family problems, medical expenses, accidents, crime, etc.)[8]

8. "A survey of 10,000 teenagers by the Center for Study of Social Behavior in North Carolina found that 10 percent were heavy drinkers and nearly a third were moderate to heavy-moderate drinkers."[9] "By the time they graduate from high school . . . more than half of the country's young people will drink at least weekly."[10]

9. Statistics of motor vehicle departments in a significant number of states reveal that, when the legal age for drinking was reduced from twenty-one to eighteen, the number of fatal accidents on the highway increased materially. An independent study by the University of Chicago Law School bore out this trend.

Now back to the biblical materials and an attempt to find help there.

What About Other Parts of the Bible Besides Proverbs?

In both the Old and the New Testaments excessive eating and drinking are roundly condemned. For example, Isaiah 5:11-12 reads "You are doomed! You get up early in the morning to start drinking, and you spend long evenings getting drunk. At your feasts you have harps and tambourines and flutes—and wine. . . ."

In Matthew 11:19 and Luke 7:34 we read that Jesus was accused of being "a glutton and wine-drinker." Wine production was a leading industry in Palestine then (and is in Israel today), and everybody drank wine. It is interesting that in both Testaments there are both praise and condemnation of wine. Psalm 104:15 speaks of its pleasure-producing properties. Also, it had a place in the sacrificial system (Exodus 29:40, etc.). But drinking to the point of intoxication was regarded as disgraceful; Genesis 9:20-27 (Noah), Genesis 19:31-

[7] Thomas F. A. Plaut, "Addiction: Alcohol," in *Encyclopedia of Social Work, Seventeenth Issue,* ed., John B. Turner et al. (Washington, D.C.: National Association of Social Workers, 1977), vol. 1, p. 22.

[8] R. C. Berry, J. P. Boland, C. N. Smart, and J. R. Kavak, *Further Analysis of the Economic Costs of Alcohol Abuse and Alcoholism,* 1977. For the National Institute on Alcohol Abuse and Alcoholism.

[9] *Boston Globe,* Nov. 27, 1977.

[10] Berry, Boland, Smart, and Kavak, *op. cit.*

38 (Lot), Jeremiah 13:13, and Ezekiel 23:33 are worth looking up. Drinking was seen as robbing people of their senses and leading to licentious living (Hosea 4:11, 18). Micah claimed that the people were clamoring for a preacher who would predict plenty of liquor for all (Micah 2:11). According to the prophets, it could produce moral blindness (read the devastating words about intoxicated priests and prophets in Isaiah 28:7, and about drinking on the part of the nation's leaders in Isaiah 56:12!). Priests were not to drink any wine at all when on duty (Leviticus 10:8-9), And two groups—the Nazirites (Numbers 6:3) and, later, the Rechabites (Jeremiah 35:6-7) were forbidden ever to touch it.

In the New Testament, drunkards are not to be put up with in the Christian community (1 Corinthians 5:11-13). This kind of living reflected Gentile depravity. Drunkards would not inherit the kingdom (1 Corinthians 6:10; Galatians 5:21; 1 Peter 4:3). So we find in Romans 13:13, "Let us conduct ourselves properly, as people who live in the light of day no orgies or drunkenness. . . ." And in special reference to the clergy, intemperance should never be countenanced in a bishop (1 Timothy 3:3, Titus 1:7).

WHAT DO YOU DO WITH 1 TIMOTHY 5:23?

Since this is a DO-IT-YOURSELF chapter, ask yourself what this really says, to how many it was addressed, and why.

How Do You Yourself Come Out on All This?

Are you now ready, after working through the preceding pages, to write down *three* conclusions to which you have come with regard to the Christian's eating and drinking? Please write them down:

1. _____

2. _____

3. _____

And for the final word: "Whether you eat or drink . . . do all to the glory of God (1 Corinthians 10:31, RSV).

What Some Others Have Said

"Nothing to excess."—Inscription in the Temple of Apollo at Delphi.

"Tell me what you eat, and I will tell you what you are."—Jean Anthelme Brillat-Savarin, *Physiologie du Goût,* 1825; many translations under the title *Physiology of Taste.*

"Licker talks mighty loud w'en it git loose from de jug."—Joel Chandler Harris, *Uncle Remus, His Songs and Sayings,* 1890.

"Thou shouldst eat to live, not live to eat."—Cicero, *Rhetoricorum.*

"The innkeeper loves the drunkard, but not for a son-in-law."—Yiddish proverb.

"If you wish to grow thinner, diminish your dinner. . . ."—Henry Sambrooke Leigh, *A Day for Wishing,* 1868.

"Where the drink goes in, there the wit goes out."—George Herbert (1593–1633), *Jacula Prudentum.*

"I eat to live, to serve, and also, if it so happens, to enjoy, but I do not eat for the sake of enjoyment."—Mohandas Karamchand Gandhi, as quoted in Franklin Pierce Adams, *FPA Book of Quotations,* 1952.

"Middle-aged rabbits don't have a paunch, do have their own teeth, and haven't lost their romantic appeal."—Dr. Aurelia Poter, *The New York Times,* Sept. 22, 1956.

"I have often marveled at the fact that so many large Eastern businesses are headed by Western boys. Is it because the son of a well-to-do Eastern family is exposed to social temptations which sap his energies and dull his perceptions . . .? A debutante party is certainly not a fitting prelude to a busy day, nor is a night at the Stork Club. The Western boy at work in New York, bolstered, perhaps, by a little quiet homework, keen and fresh each morning, has proved himself tough competition for the man who wears the club tie."—Robert R. Young, Chairman of the Board, New York Central Railroad, in a graduation address, 1955. Quoted in *Newsweek,* June 20, 1955.

Hot Tempers
and How to
Control Them Better

> *"If religion does nothing for your temper it has done nothing for your soul."* [1]

If you never get angry, don't bother to read any further. That is, unless, of course, you can tactfully help your youngster or a good friend.

—WARNING—

It is much easier to deal with someone else's bad temper than with our own.

Some Nagging Questions

Let's start with a few down-to-earth questions that jump into our minds right off.

✓ Isn't it sometimes better to "blow off steam" and "let it go" than to keep angry feelings all bottled up inside?

✓ Why do some people have much hotter tempers than others?

✓ Didn't Jesus himself get angry (Mark 3:5 and the implications of Mark 11:15-17)?

✓ Don't some parents feel that something is wrong if a child doesn't "throw a tantrum" now and then?

✓ Why does the Bible say so much about the anger (wrath) of God?

✓ Does it seem easier to control outer space than inner?

✓ What is your own boiling point?

[1] Robert Clayton, Irish Bishop (1695–1758).

What Do You Find in Proverbs (plenty)

Be sure to read these passages in your favorite translation:

14:17 suggests that when we get angry, we do foolish things that we wouldn't do when calm.

14:29—A hot temper is a sign of stupidity!

15:1—"A gentle answer quiets anger"; read the rest of the verse.

15:18—"Hot tempers cause arguments. . . ." (Don't we know it!) The verse recommends what?

16:32—Controlling a bad temper is one of the greatest of achievements!

17:27b—This speaks about a person who manages to keep calm.

19:11—Hanging on to one's temper is the mark of a sensible person.

19:19—If you do, you'll take the consequences!

21:14—"If someone is angry with you, a gift given secretly will calm him down." (Why secretly?)

22:24, 25—Those who "pal around" with people with violent tempers may become just like them!

27:4—Anger can be cruel and destructive (we've found that out).

29:11 resembles 14:29.

29:22 is much like 15:18a.

30:33—Anger causes scraps!

(And did we miss some?)

"The Thirty Wise Sayings"

In the *Good News Bible,* 22:17 reads, "Listen, and I will teach you what wise men have said. Study their teachings." Chapter 22, verse 19b says, "That is why I am going to tell them to you now." See the rendering in the *New English Bible, Jerusalem Bible,* and especially the *New American Bible.* If you are interested in an apparent reference to thirty sayings which a now-famous Egyptian scribe wrote to guide his children in their careers, see chapter 4, p. 40.

What happens to a person when he/she gets angry? The Hebrew of Genesis 30:2 is very expressive: literally, "his nose became hot." That is, he got angry. Deuteronomy 13:17 calls anger a "burning of the nose." We use similar expressions when we speak of a "red-hot temper" or of a person getting "hot under the collar."

We do not have space here to go into the matter of the "wrath" of God; it is very important, and it would be worth your while to consult one or two good Bible dictionaries.

Magazine Articles?

To move along, note how prevalent is the concern which temper causes, by looking in our popular magazines. Here are some titles of articles: "How to Be an Angry Mother"; "How to Be Good, and Mad"; "Emotional First Aid?"; "How to Cool Your Anger"; "Express Anger, Lower Anxiety"; "Letting Your Anger Work for You"; and "A 3-Step Guide to Resolving Anger Constructively."

Before starting to tie the loose ends together with some practical suggestions, let's note four passages from the New Testament.

From the Gospels, "But now I tell you: whoever is angry [the best manuscripts do not have "without a cause" as in the King James Version] with his brother will be brought to trial, whoever calls his brother 'You good-for-nothing!' will be brought before the Council [Sanhedrin], and whoever calls his brother a worthless fool will be in danger of going to the fire of hell" (Matthew 5:22). What does this mean? In Matthew 5:21-48 our Lord is deepening the old Law to include attitudes as well as acts. He strongly emphasizes that angry feelings and contemptuous words are wrong, dead wrong, as well as criminal acts like murder!

What about the rest of the New Testament? Ephesians 4:31-32 reads, "Get rid of all bitterness, passion, and anger. No shouting or insults, no more hateful feelings of any sort. Instead, be kind and tender-hearted to one another, and forgive one another, as God has forgiven you through Christ." And Colossians 3:8 says, "But now you must get rid of all these things: anger, passion, and hateful feelings. No insults or obscene talk must ever come from your lips." But the writer is realistic and knows frail human nature: "If you become angry, do not let your anger lead you into sin, and do not stay angry all day." The King James Version reads: "Let not the sun go down upon your wrath" (Ephesians 4:26).

Someone is surely thinking about the matter of "righteous" anger, sometimes termed "righteous indignation." This is not the fiery temper which is being discussed in Proverbs. But it is surely found in the pages of Scripture; the honest reader of the Gospels knows that Jesus was angry, very angry at the abuses in the religious system of his time, at crippling demonic forces, at debilitating unbelief, as well as at the millionaire ring of Sadducees which had cornered the market on the sale of sacrificial animals and the making of change for the temple tax. We call this righteous anger; it is real anger just the same, but quite different from the tantrum variety.

Practical Help

Many years ago William James gave three pieces of advice to those attempting to root out one habit and to replace it with another:
1. Launch out with a strong initiative.
2. Don't allow any exception until the new habit is well rooted.
3. Take the first possible opportunity to act on your resolution.[2]

Twelve Practical Suggestions

1. Recognize the problem. How often do you explode? What are the things which are most likely to set you off in a fit of anger? What is your boiling point?

2. When you are on the verge of letting go, try to delay the outburst. Thomas Jefferson advised, "When you are angry, count ten before you speak; if very angry, a hundred."[3] And a certain Athenodorus counseled Caesar Augustus, "Remember, when you are angry, to say or do nothing until you have repeated the four-and-twenty letters [of the alphabet] to yourself."[4]

3. Try taking your anger out on an inanimate object in a non-destructive way and preferably where you won't be seen. A friend who lived in China before the revolution told the writer of seeing women going out of their homes and completely disappearing from circulation for a short time. What were they doing? They would go to the city wall, alone, where nobody could see or hear, and "give it" to the wall—"let the wall have it." Then they would return, with the hot feelings out of their systems. Some people hit a pillow, kick on a bed, scream in a parked car in a deserted spot where no one hears. Others play the piano *fortissimo* (if other tenants are away) or flail away at a punching bag. Anger can thus be funneled into harmless channels.

4. If possible, turn your attention to something else. Get your mind off the thing or person that makes you so angry.

5. Ask God's help as quickly as possible. This will become a habit eventually for the moment when "the temperature starts shooting up."

6. If your temper is really of the red-hot variety, your resolution about handling it better should not only be a mental one, but also should be written down on paper and carried about where you have to see it periodically. Communicate to someone that you've made the

[2] See his *Principles of Psychology,* 1890.
[3] Thomas Jefferson, *Writings,* vol. xvi, p. 111.
[4] Plutarch, *Lives,* "Caesar Augustus."

solemn resolution and that you really mean business. Would it help to read it aloud periodically?

7. Have real confidence that God and you can raise your boiling point.

8. At the end of the week make a serious review of the past seven days. On what days did you really "make it" with flying colors? Epictetus, first-century Stoic philosopher, urged people to say, "I used to be angry every day; now every other day; then every third and fourth day. And if you miss it so long as thirty days, offer a sacrifice of thanksgiving to God."[5]

9. Don't go to bed at night nursing anger. Take time to read Ephesians 4:26 in three recent translations.

10. Keep, so far as you can, out of situations where you are most likely to explode. But many times that will not be possible. However, don't let your failures discourage you. Don't make excuses for them; just admit them. Then, asking God's forgiveness and help, start over again. And be very thankful to him every time you succeed.

William Barclay says that a friend of his met a man who had had a tremendous struggle with temper. "I see," said Barclay's friend, "that you have succeeded in conquering your temper." "No," said the man, "I didn't conquer it. Jesus conquered it for me."[6]

What Some Others Have Said

"A man should study ever to keep cool. He makes his inferiors his superiors by heat."—Ralph Waldo Emerson, *Uncollected Lectures: Social Aims,* delivered Dec. 4, 1864.

"Anyone can become angry—that is easy, but to be angry with the right person, to the right degree, at the right time, for the right purpose, and in the right way—that . . . is not easy."—Aristotle, *Nichomachean Ethics,* 335 B.C.

"The size of a man can be measured by the size of the thing that makes him angry."—J. Kenfield Morley, *Some Things I Believe,* 1937.

"Bridle your tongue and you saddle your temper."—Howard K. Jerome, *Reflections of a Bachelor,* 1911.

[5] Epictetus, *Discourses,* book ii, ch. 18.
[6] William Barclay, *The Gospel of Luke,* rev. ed. (Philadelphia: The Westminster Press, 1975), p. 105.

"A man in a passion rides a mad horse."—Benjamin Franklin, *Poor Richard's Almanack,* December, 1749.

"The one that fust gits mad 's most ollers wrong."—James Russell Lowell, *Bigelow Papers,* 1848.

"Anger is an expensive luxury in which only men of a certain income can indulge."—George William Curtis, *Prue and I,* 1857.

12

The Fear of
the Lord:
What Does It Mean?

Are you wondering about this word "fear"? Think of all the fears there are in the world; here is a partial list from the dictionary:

acrophobia—fear of high places
agoraphobia—fear of open spaces
aichinophobia—fear of sharp objects
ailurophobia—fear of cats
androphobia—fear of men
apeirophobia—fear of infinity
astraphobia—fear of thunderstorms
autophobia—fear of self, of being alone
ballistophobia—fear of missiles
bathophobia—fear of depths
chionophobia—fear of snow
claustrophobia—fear of confined places
cynophobia—fear of dogs
demophobia—fear of crowds
erythrophobia—fear of red
gamophobia—fear of marriage
gynophobia—fear of women
haptophobia—fear of being touched
hemophobia—fear of blood
hydrophobia—fear of water
kinesophobia—fear of movement
lalophobia—fear of speaking

musophobia—fear of mice
mysophobia—fear of contamination
necrophobia—fear of dead bodies
neophobia—fear of new things
nyctophobia—fear of night, darkness
ophidiophobia—fear of reptiles
pedophobia—fear of infants or children
phagophobia—fear of eating
phonophobia—fear of noise
photophobia—fear of light
psychrophobia—fear of cold
pyrophobia—fear of fire
taphephobia—fear of being buried alive
thalassophobia—fear of ocean or sea
thanatophobia—fear of death
toxicophobia—fear of poison
zoophobia—fear of animals[1]

Perhaps you can add some more.

Some famous people have confessed to some terrible fears. Erasmus was terrified at the sight of a fish. Newton and Paganini both were afraid of a basin of water. Schumann, Chopin, and Poe feared fog. And de Maupassant was terribly afraid of an open door, afraid that the nameless thing, madness, would enter—and it did, at last.

But What About the "Fear of the Lord"?

See how often this phrase occurs in the book of Proverbs, beginning at 1:7, the motto of the book ("The fear of the Lord is the beginning of knowledge" [KJV and RSV]). And it occurs eighteen more times before the book is done. Please take four or five minutes to look these passages up:

1:29
2:5
3:7
8:13
9:10
10:27 Do you agree completely?

[1] *Reader's Digest Great Encyclopedic Dictionary* (Pleasantville, N.Y.: The Reader's Digest Association, 1966), p. 1014.

14:2, 26, 27
15:16, 33
16:6*b* ⎫
19:23 ⎬ Are these always true as you watch life?
22:4 ⎭
23:17
24:21 Is there a difference between the way one fears God and the way he fears the king?
28:14
31:30

What about fear in religion? Take time to go into this subject without hurrying.

In the year 1741, a famous sermon was preached in Northampton, Massachusetts, entitled "Sinners in the Hands of an Angry God." The minister was the famous and learned Jonathan Edwards. People fainted as lurid pictures were painted of people dangling over the fires of hell. But before you brush this off as the product of a bygone era, ask yourself some questions. Do you really want to see ALL fear ruled out of life?

Think about a small child. When I was four or five years old, we were playing a game which involved forfeits. Not dreaming that I would do it, someone jokingly told me to kiss the kitchen stove. I did. Fortunately, it was not very hot. So, aren't there a lot of things which we train our children to be afraid of, like running out into the street when traffic is thick, like bottles with high-powered medicine, and sharp tools, especially ones that are powered?

Move along to the teenager. Aren't there some things of which you'd like to feel that your teenaged son or daughter has a real fear? Name three.

And now think of ourselves. Isn't there something to say in favor of *everybody's* having a real, healthy fear of doing the second-best things and living the second-best kind of life, storing up regrets for the tag-end years?

WHAT ABOUT IT?

Are we really going to abandon all fear *in religion?* We'd better go back to see what the book of Proverbs has to say. Would you be surprised to find out that words for fear, awe, dread, and the like occur several hundred times throughout the Old Testament; that there are over twenty Hebrew words to denote them; and that the New Testament has over a hundred references to such emotions?

The first thing one discovers is that the words for fear and related feelings are intensely agitating, highly charged words signifying the deepest sensations. Terrien writes, "Fear, distress, and dismay are thus suggested by many different words which mean trembling, quaking, shaking, quivering, shuddering, staggering, reeling, hair-bristling, palpitating, writhing, twirling, whirling, etc."[2]

But the commonest word, *yir'āh,* a form of which appears in the term "fear of the Lord," is to be distinguished clearly from other words which signify terror, dismay, and anxiety. Let us lay down several propositions.

1. Fear in the Old Testament is the result of the sense of *the immense distance between puny man and Almighty God, qualitatively speaking.* Eichrodt writes, ". . . the sense of the gap between God and Man [is] the dominant element in Old Testament piety. . . .[3] (Do you ever feel a trifle resentful when overfamiliar, almost possessive prayers are addressed to the Creator and Ruler of the universe?)

> For my thoughts are not your
>   thoughts,
>   neither are your ways my ways,
>   says the LORD.
> For as the heavens are higher than
>   the earth,
>   so are my ways higher than your
>   ways
>   and my thoughts than your thoughts.
>   (Isaiah 55:8-9, RSV)

2. Yet the infinite greatness of God, while it agitates one deeply, does not terrify so much as it attracts us, mystifies us, and fills us with awe. So Jacob, when he awoke at Bethel feeling unmistakably the presence of God, was shaking with fear as he said, "Surely the Lord is in this place; and I did not know it. . . . How awesome. . . . This is none other than the house of God, and this is the gate of heaven"

---

[2] Samuel Terrien, "Fear," in *Interpreter's Dictionary of the Bible,* ed. G. A. Buttrick (Nashville: Abingdon Press, 1962), vol. 2, p. 257.

[3] Walter Eichrodt, *Theology of the Old Testament,* trans. J. A. Baker (Philadelphia: The Westminster Press, 1961), vol. 2, p. 268.

(Genesis 28:16-17, RSV). But he goes on to approach God for protection and assistance. "If God will be with me, and will keep me . . . and give me bread to eat and clothing to wear . . . then . . . I will give the tenth to thee" (28:20, 22, RSV).

3. The fear of God *was not a feeling of terror (as it was in some other religions) because God communicated himself to his people as a covenant God.* So fear becomes reverent awe. But do not tone it down beyond this! God is "majestic in holiness, terrible in glorious deeds" (Exodus 15:11, RSV), mysterious, powerful, and yet the God who has a great purpose for his people (Genesis 12:2, 3) and who, therefore, commands respect, obedience, adventurous trust, and love.

Now we are ready to go to the motto of the book of Proverbs. Chapter 1, verse 7 reads, "The fear of the Lord is the beginning of knowledge" (KJV and RSV). Try several other translations. Scott in the *Anchor Bible* translates it, "The first principle of knowledge is to hold the Lord in awe."

Out of this we get a strong sense that the deepest reverence for God is a giant step in acquiring true education.

BUT WHAT IS REAL REVERENCE?

Let's illustrate it with two incidents. Years ago the famous Baron von Hügel was walking on a beautiful moonlit night on the Wiltshire Downs of England with a younger companion. Suddenly, as he gazed at the magnificent display of stars, he forgot his friend and in tones of deep emotion simply said, "God, God, God!"[4]

And the second: Ask yourself how far ahead an American who is to be presented at the court of St. James, that is, to meet Queen Elizabeth II personally, begins to prepare. Months are spent on what is to be worn, what is to be done, what is to be said. SHOULD WE NOT BE AS CONCERNED to enter the presence of Almighty God in a fitting way? (How do *you* enter the sanctuary on Sunday morning?)

A religion without reverence is a contradiction! So an adult class of which the author was privileged to be the teacher prepared these ten down-to-earth suggestions as to how to practice reverence as one comes to the sanctuary for worship:

1. I will not wait until 10 A.M. on Sunday to ask myself what I am doing here. I'll try to begin to prepare myself on Saturday evening, and when I get up on Sunday, I will develop some real expectations

[4] *The Observer,* Sunday, June 13, 1937, p. 9. Quoted in John H. Scammon, *Living with the Psalms* (Valley Forge, Pa.: Judson Press, 1967), p. 138.

that I'm going to get real answers and a real experience.

2. Of course, God is everywhere, but I need a special place where the world's noise is muffled and I can find his Presence. So when the organ prelude begins, I'll look around less and look up more. This place where I am is a house of God.

3. When I am first seated, I'll quietly pray for myself, for each person around me, and for those in the world who have no one to pray for them.

4. I'll try to pay a lot more attention to the words of the hymns I sing, trying to feel what circumstances might have caused the authors to write them.

5. I will listen to the reading of the Scripture as if it were addressed to me in a personal letter. I'll try to see the people described, watch them move about, hear their voices rise and fall. Perhaps God will speak to me through his written word as much as in the sermon.

6. I'll work hard to listen to every word of the anthems, realizing that God may have a real uplift for me at this point. I am grateful that the words are often printed in the calendar for me to follow.

7. As I put my offering in the plate (and I'll have it fixed up beforehand), I'll remember all that has been done for me in my lifetime, especially by God. And I'll use the time of the offering as a rededication not only of my money but also of myself to the work of Jesus Christ on this earth.

8. I will not think of how much good the sermon would do for someone else; I'll listen for God's word in it for me. As my minister begins to preach, I'll pray for him.

9. I will watch for a refocusing of the sermon's message in the sermon prayer and the closing hymn.

10. And when I get up to leave, I'll try to carry home one thing to live by this week.

What Some Others Have Said

"The greatest question of our time is not communism versus individualism, not Europe versus America, not even the East versus the West; it is whether man can bear to live without God."—Will Durant, *On the Meaning of Life,* 1932.

"It is a law of man's nature, written into his very essence, and just as much a part of him as the desire to build houses and cultivate the land and marry and have children and read books and sing songs, that he should want to stand together with other men in order to acknowledge their common dependence on God, their Father and Creator."—Thomas Merton, *The Seven Storey Mountain,* 1948.

"The course of human history consists of a series of encounters between individual human beings and God in which each man and woman or child, in turn, is challenged by God to make his free choice between doing God's will and refusing to do it."—Arnold J. Toynbee, *Collier's,* March 30, 1956.

"The way to success in this great country, with its fair judgments, is to show that you are not afraid of anybody except God and His final verdict."—Woodrow Wilson, address in Philadelphia, July 4, 1914.

13

The Planned, Thought-Out Life

> *I want to live, live out, not wobble through*
> *My life somehow, and then into the dark.*[1]

In the Introduction to this book we said, "The book [of Proverbs] is heavy on the necessity of a planned, thought out life, a quality so often lacking today." The real question now is: Granted that we want to do some planning, what *can* be planned, and what *can't?*

We begin with the second. First, we all agree that *there are many uncertainties in the future which are not in our hands at all.* As Proverbs 27:1 says, "Never boast about tomorrow. You don't know what will happen between now and then." Let's list some uncertainties:

1. Our "time of departure" (2 Timothy 4:6)
2. Local, national, and world conditions in the future
3. The way our children and grandchildren will "pan out"

LIST SOME MORE

4. _____
5. _____
6. _____
7. _____
8. _____

[1]G. A. Studdert Kennedy, "Faith," *The Unutterable Beauty* (London: Hodder & Stoughton, Ltd., 1927), p. 5.

As Proverbs 16:1 puts it, "Men may make their plans, but God has the last word."

BUT

There certainly are SOME THINGS where planning *can make a big difference.* Let's put it bluntly: your last will and testament makes plans for your death; what plans do you have for the rest of your life? We go to our doctor for annual *medical* checkups; we see the dentist for checks on our teeth. What about taking a little time right now for a *spiritual* check? DON'T PLAY THE REST OF YOUR LIFE BY CHANCE!

So, exactly what can we plan?

1. *We can select the highway we travel on.* Proverbs 4:18 puts it, "The road the righteous travel is like the sunrise, getting brighter and brighter until daylight has come."

Dr. Roy Menninger, president of the Menninger Foundation in Topeka, Kansas, made an unusual suggestion in the course of an address not very long ago:

> "If you want to find out where you stand in life, sit down and write your obituary. As you write it, you'll have to decide what to say about yourself. What kind of person you are. What you want to be remembered for. Will you be remembered only because you had three houses, two cars, and a boat? Or will you be remembered for the kind of person you were? Middle age is usually when you suddenly realize that you're not going to win the Nobel prize. You're not going to be the richest man in Kansas City or president of the Chamber of Commerce. It's that time when we face the reality that we are human—that we have limits. . . ."[2]

Think how clearly any sizable obituary indicates the road the person has traveled. Would you be willing to sit at your desk or table FOR TEN MINUTES and write an obituary for yourself the way you'd like to have it printed some day? It would be a very interesting and worthwhile project.

T. R. Glover wrote that a life based on God has four things: sanity, reserve, composure, and steadiness.[3] Proverbs 14:26 reads, "Reverence for the LORD gives confidence and security to a man and his family." Do you agree?

Those of us who are trying very hard to be Christian may well be able to remember a day and an hour when we deliberately chose the

2Copyrighted by the Menninger Foundation.

3T. R. Glover, *The Jesus of History* (Folcroft, Pa.: Folcroft Press, 1917), p. 61. He quotes these four but does not indicate source.

highway we wanted to travel on the rest of our lives. The author still has that tiny diary for 1917 (when he was "just a kid") with a brief entry for Sunday, March 25: "Went to church, Sunday School, Junior Christian Endeavor. Took stand in J.C.E." That afternoon in a back room in my father's church when a woman, the evangelist's assistant, challenged the small group of boys and girls to put up a hand to signify a real love for Jesus, an eleven-year-old boy did so with tears. Three months later he was baptized. *And he has never regretted that decision.*

> "To every man there openeth
> A Way, and Ways, and a Way.
>
> . . . .
>
> And every man decideth
> The Way his soul shall go."[4]

Perhaps this *should make more difference in the way we divide our time.*

Someone suggests this: "If one lives to be seventy years of age and is the average person, he spends

> twenty three years sleeping,
> nineteen years working,
> nine years playing,
> six years eating,
> six years traveling,
> two years dressing,
> four years unaccounted for,

AND, one year in the house of the Lord . . . if he worships regularly."

Try making a chart of your time, dividing a circle into pieces representing, as accurately as possible, that part of the twenty-four hours of an average day which you spend in

1. Eating
2. Working on the job, including time spent going and coming
3. Sleeping
4. Recreation
5. Reading the newspaper or books
6. Watching TV
7. Doing things with your family

---

[4] John Oxenham, "The Ways," *Gentlemen—The King!* (Philadelphia: Pilgrim Press, 1928). Reprinted by permission of Theo Oxenham and The Pilgrim Press. Copyright 1928 John Oxenham; copyright renewed 1956 Erica Oxenham.

8. Attending church, fraternal organizations, and any other significant items. Please spend ten minutes working this out:

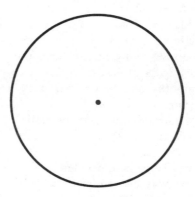

How do you feel about the chart?

Then, too, *possibly we can do better with some area of our life in the light of the preceding chapters.* The author would be grateful if God uses some of them; he freely confesses that making the study has done him good. I'm sure that most of us are aware that never before have there been so many fine agencies at work, all needing hours and money.

Finally *we might well reconsider the priorities of our lives.* Here is a striking paragraph from a friend's sermon; he says:

> I have a friend who lives in England. During the war he resided in one of England's most frequently bombed communities. He told me of a particular day when enemy planes were overhead, dropping their cargoes of death and destruction. Whole streets were ablaze. The authorities ordered the people to evacuate the city. My friend said, "It is a revealing experience to step into the home which you have known and loved for many years, every room filled with precious memories, and know that within five minutes you have to choose what you want to save. You look at your belongings which you have acquired over the years by search and sacrifice—books, pictures, souvenirs, rugs, chairs, ornaments—everything that goes into making a home. Home—and the flames are only one hundred yards away! You know that you will never see the place again. Then you realize that all you can take to represent a life-time of living are the few things that you and your wife can gather up in your two hands. You walk from room to room. Suddenly you realize that the choice is not as difficult as you had expected . . . My wife and I picked up a few pictures of our loved ones, some precious letters, one or two books of poetry that were dear to us, a cup that we had used for drinking at a spring when we were on our honeymoon, and the Bible which we read daily. They did not fill the

little handbag that I carried. And then we hurried out. We walked down the road as the flames were blistering the walls of our house. And we had with us everything that we deemed most precious out of a whole life-time of living. Everything that we left behind was consumed within thirty minutes."[5]

But they had one other thing—their Christian faith! As a wonderful Christian friend wrote to me some years ago:

> It seems to me that what people need most of all today is again to feel caught up in God's purpose, a part of His plan, used by Him to forward His Kingdom. Once you begin to feel that, you take on a new stature, life has a new importance, and you want to begin fitting yourself to be worthy of such a role. Wouldn't that take care of a lot of the neuroses so prevalent today?[6]

WHAT A GLORIOUS THING A PLANNED, THOUGHT-OUT LIFE OF THIS KIND CAN BE! See John 8:36.

What do you think about it for yourself?

What Some Others Have Said

"The life which is unexamined is not worth living."—Plato, *Apology*.

"If you don't know where you're going, any road will get you there."—Salada Tea tag line. Used by permission of the Kellogg Company.

"'Better than other people.' Sometimes he says, 'That, at least, you are.' But more often: 'Why should you be? Either you are what you can be, or if you are not. . . .'"—Dag Hammerskjöld, *Markings*, 1964.

Many years ago Horace Bushnell preached a famous sermon, "Every Man's Life a Plan of God."

"Talking last week with some relatives and friends around a table of refreshments, we heard one of them tell of a close call he had had not long before. He was at a lakeside as a storm started rumbling up over the lake, complete with lightning flashes. One of the bolts struck the lake, ricocheted off, hit the car, and knocked the car keys out of his hand as he was about to apply them to the lock. The keys were still warm when he recovered from his fright, picked them up, opened the door, and sat down at length in the safety of his car with a great sense

[5] Sermon, "If You Had Only Five Minutes," preached by Dr. Frederick M. Meek at Old South Church, Boston, Massachusetts, January 28, 1951. Used by permission.
[6] Personal letter from Mrs. Harriet Miller.

of awe and relief. 'It made me realize that we can't ever take being alive for granted,' he said, 'and it made me take another look at my life to see if I was making the most of it.'"—John R. Schroeder.

"What can you do? You can furnish one Christian life!"—Phillips Brooks.

"Give the best that you have to the highest you know—and do it now."—Ralph W. Sockman, "On Achieving Goals," 1952.

Appendix **A**
Fifty English Proverbs
Collected by Marguerite Estaver

1. A fool and his money are soon parted.
2. A tree that bends does not break.
3. If it rained porridge, his bowl would be upside down
4. It takes a big man to fill a big man's shoes.
5. Do not count your chickens before they hatch.
6. There is no use crying over spilled milk.
7. A blind ox falls into the ditch.
8. Little kittens make big cats.
9. The long nose may get snipped off.
10. Any song that begins also ends.
11. Fields look green a long way off.
12. It is darkest just before the dawn.
13. When you are at the bottom, there is only one way to go—up.
14. A chain is only as strong as its weakest link.
15. A young fool makes many, but an old fool is the worst of any.
16. What gets your attention gets you.
17. Even the devil can quote Scripture for his purpose.
18. Being sorry doesn't pay the fiddler.
19. Satan has some mischief still for idle hands to do.
20. It is the empty wagon that makes the most noise.
21. He who laughs last laughs best.

22. A bird in the hand is worth two in the bush.
23. It is a long road that has no turning.
24. To marry in haste is to repent at your leisure.
25. Be not penny-wise and pound-foolish.
26. Water does not run uphill.
27. It takes a thief to catch a thief.
28. A stitch in time saves nine.
29. He who laughs before breakfast will cry before supper.
30. The river that twists takes longer to arrive.
31. The horse with the steady gait travels faster.
32. Time waits for no man.
33. Beware of the wolf in sheep's clothing.
34. He who hits first hits hardest.
35. A mother's love, deeper than hell.
36. All who cry are not sorry.
37. To lock the barn door after the horse is stolen is useless.
38. Look before you leap.
39. What isn't said can't come back to hurt.
40. Haste makes waste.
41. That's water under the bridge.
42. Honesty is the best policy.
43. A friend in need is a friend indeed.
44. Familiarity breeds contempt.
45. Tomorrow is never yet.
46. Handsome is as handsome does.
47. The fool rushes in where angels fear to tread.
48. A rose is just as sweet by another name.
49. A watched kettle never boils.
50. Your actions speak so loud I can't hear what you say.

Appendix B
Fifty Proverbs
from Other Cultures

1. One day a guest, two days a guest, three days a nuisance. (East Indian)
2. Four things are difficult to hide: fire, the itch, a cough, and love. (Polish)
3. A new broom sweeps clean, but the old brush knows the corners. (Irish)
4. He who can't write says the pen is bad. (Yiddish)
5. He who has no fire in himself cannot warm others. (Swiss-German)
6. Eyes to see with, ears to hear with, and a mouth to keep silence. (Chilean)
7. A fertile field, if it doesn't rest, becomes sterile. (Argentine)
8. There is nothing so eloquent as a rattlesnake's tail. (American Indian)
9. When might takes charge, justice withdraws. (Japanese)
10. To be a man is easy; to play the man is hard. (Chinese)
11. Time is anger's medicine. (German)
12. He prepares evil for himself who plots mischief for others. (Latin)
13. If you fear that people will know, don't do it. (Chinese)
14. People count up the faults of those who keep them waiting. (French)
15. Two ears to one tongue; therefore, hear twice as much as you speak. (Greek)

16. When one door is shut, another opens. (Spanish)
17. If you believe everything you read, better not read. (Japanese)
18. The morning glories aren't particularly lovely to a man with the backache. (Black)
19. No put yourself in barrel when match-box can hold you. (Jamaican)
20. It is not enough for a man to know how to ride; he must know how to fall. (Mexican)
21. There is no better friend than a burden. (Columbian)
22. No one has so big a house that he does not need a good neighbor. (Swedish)
23. An untouched drum does not speak. (Liberian)
24. When the sun rises, it rises for everyone. (Cuban)
25. You can't prevent bird from flying over your head, but you can prevent him making nest in your head. (Jamaican)
26. When the bait is worth more than the fish, 'tis time to stop fishing. (Black)
27. One doth not get good things when one saith evil things. (Egyptian)
28. Nobody's family can hang out the sign, "Nothing the matter here." (Chinese)
29. First the man takes a drink, then the drink takes a drink, then the drink takes the man. (Japanese)
30. A man without a smiling face must not open shop. (Chinese)
31. When you bow, bow low. (Chinese)
32. A runaway monk never praises his convent. (Italian)
33. It is better to be poor with honor than rich with shame. (German)
34. Muddy springs will have muddy streams. (Italian)
35. Where there is no good within, no good comes out. (Dutch)
36. Marry and grow tame. (Portuguese)
37. He who fears to suffer, suffers from fear. (French)
38. You can't clap with one palm. (Chinese)
39. When you leave a country, you leave behind something of your heart. (Belgian)
40. Half an orange tastes as sweet as the whole one. (Chinese)
41. A great city, a great solitude. (Greek)

42. The best apples float on the top of the peck measure. (Black)
43. Everyone gives a shove to the tumbling wall. (Chinese)
44. If I had not lifted up the stone, you had not found the jewel. (Jewish)
45. Ill comes upon war's back. (Scottish)
46. Bad news always comes too soon. (German)
47. He that never fails never grows rich. (Italian)
48. Borrowing brings care. (Dutch)
49. Let him eat the tough morsel who eats the tender. (Portuguese)
50. It is easy to frighten a bull from the window. (Italian)

Appendix C
A Twelve-Inch Shelf
of Books to Help

In case you'd like further help on the book of Proverbs, here is a small shelf of less technical books to which you can go back again and again. You may in certain cases wish to substitute other titles; however, the following have proved useful to many students. There is room at the end of the list for you to add others.

First of all, on your shelf there needs to be *the text* of Proverbs in a good, reliable translation and in the language of today. Why the latter? We reiterate that the King James Version (1611) is the most beautiful one you'll ever read, but the best, oldest, longest biblical manuscripts have all been discovered since then, involving some changes; further, 850 words found in the King James Version have changed their meaning in 350-plus years. Many of you use the Revised Standard Version (1952), but you'd better, in addition, choose one of the following *colloquial* translations (in the best sense: the way we speak TODAY):

1. *Good News Bible* (1976). A very handy, inexpensive paperback of Proverbs and Ecclesiastes, entitled *Wisdom for Modern Man,* is published by the American Bible Society.

2. *The Living Bible* (1971); this, according to the subtitle, is a paraphrase rather than a translation and should be read as such.

3. *The New English Bible* (1961)

4. *The Jerusalem Bible* (1966)

5. *The New American Bible* (1970).

If you'd like to consult a translation which will tell you, very literally,

111

how the Hebrew or the Greek says it, dip into the *New American Standard Bible* (1963–1971); in fact, it is *too* literal to be a great translation.

Next you need a reliable commentary. My first choice is R. B. Y. Scott's *Proverbs, Ecclesiastes* in the Anchor Bible series. For a briefer one try the excellent little volume by J. C. Rylaarsdam, *The Proverbs, Ecclesiastes, The Song of Solomon,* in The Layman's Bible Commentary set. Or if your time is very limited, try the *Interpreter's One-Volume Commentary on the Bible,* or a study Bible like the *Oxford Annotated,* or the *Jerusalem* or *New American Bible.* Just recently an annotated edition of the *New English Bible* has appeared.

Then get a concordance. (Abridged ones always seem to lack the word for which you're looking!) This will enable you to locate all occurrences of practically all of the Bible words. Here, since the Revised Standard Concordance is quite expensive (but most useful), why not use the comparatively inexpensive *Cruden's Complete Concordance of the Old and New Testaments*? This is based on the King James Version, but you can work through this to the other translations.

Finally, a good Bible dictionary will help when you are studying *the topics* (like "lying," "money," "eating," and "the fear of the Lord") as they are used in the rest of the Bible. There are several one-volume ones; a very good example is *The New Westminster Dictionary of the Bible.*

"A man's life is often built upon a proverb."
—From the German.